On Being Stuck

On Being Stuck

*Tapping Into the
Creative Power of Writer's Block*

Laraine Herring

Shambhala
Boulder · 2016

Shambhala Publications, Inc.
4720 Walnut Street
Boulder, Colorado 80301
www.shambhala.com

FIRST EDITION
Printed in United States of America

♾ This edition is printed on acid-free paper that meets the
American National Standards Institute Z39.48 Standard.

♻ This book is printed on 30% postconsumer recycled paper.
For more information please visit www.shambhala.com.

Distributed in the United States by Penguin Random House LLC
and in Canada by Random House of Canada Ltd

Designed by Michael Russem

Library of Congress Cataloging-in-Publication Data

Names: Herring, Laraine, 1968– author.
Title: On being stuck: tapping into the creative power of
writer's block /
Laraine Herring.
Description: First edition. | Boulder: Shambhala, [2016]
Identifiers: LCCN 2015037765 | ISBN 9781611802900 (paperback)
Subjects: LCSH: Writer's block. | Authorship—Psychological
aspects. | BISAC:
LANGUAGE ARTS & DISCIPLINES / Composition & Creative
Writing. | SELF-HELP / Creativity.
Classification: LCC PN171.W74 H47 2016 | DDC 808.02019—dc23
LC record available at http://lccn.loc.gov/2015037765

for Keezel

Instead of trying to force myself into doing what I imagined I ought to be doing, I began to enquire into what I was doing.

—*Marion Milner*

Contents

Part Three: Beyond the Block

The Polar Vortex, Bats, and a Green Monkey

Just after New Year's Day 2014, I find myself stuck in the polar vortex that is engulfing most of the United States. Unprecedented and deadly cold temperatures and winter storms blanket the country. Air travel as we know it ceases. I am in the Berkshires in Lenox, Massachusetts, twenty-two hundred miles away from my high desert home, to teach a writing workshop at the Kripalu Center for Yoga & Health. Although they are well accustomed to snow and cold, these hardy New Englanders have posted orange warning signs on the doors and bulletin boards:

DANGER. EXTREME COLD.

DO NOT WALK TO YOUR CAR.

CALL US FOR A RIDE.

My home in Prescott, Arizona, is 120 miles northwest of the megalopolis of Phoenix. We sit at a little over five thousand feet. We like to think we have a winter—we call ourselves "Arizona's Christmas City," and we even truck in ice for a skating rink one weekend in December—but our winters are really more of the snow globe kind, followed quickly by warm sun and short sleeves. When the temperatures drop below 55°F, we all bring out our new parkas and faux-fur-lined winter boots. "Brrr! It's cold today," we say, wrapping our light cotton scarves around our necks, grabbing our keys with our fashionable fingerless gloved hands, and walking out into the blinding winter sun. We don't think of our breath freezing in our noses. We don't worry about the pipes in our houses. If the Berkshire folk, who wear serious, dark-colored, *actual* parkas and snow boots that require tools to remove from woolen-socked feet, are worried about the cold—well, goodness—it must be some kind of cold.

In my room, I compulsively check flight statuses. Cancelled. Cancelled. Cancelled. I'm still forty-eight hours from my flight home. It's too early for a specific update for my Albany-Chicago-Phoenix route. The weather will clear soon. It always does. For kicks, I check my transfer airport, Chicago Midway. Status: red. Delays severe. No change. No one arriving. No one leaving. Not tonight. Maybe not ever. I imagine the families lined up along the narrow corridors at Midway ready to strangle the automated voice: "Welcome to Chicago Midway Airport. Smoking is not allowed in any of the buildings. . . ." I see the line snaking into the bathroom. A fight over the last chicken nugget in all the kingdom. Luggage piled seven feet high. The whole country is stuck in the middle of their plans.

I'm not too concerned. I'm indoors in a beautiful retreat facility that was formerly a Jesuit monastery. We have heated floors, running water, yoga classes, a hot tub, a world-class spa, and three scrumptious meals a day. I love teaching this workshop, and I really do love coming to Massachusetts in the winter. The snow is a novelty for me—like trying on sexy stilettos or snorkeling. Plus, I don't have to do any of the winter work. Kripalu's facilities' team doesn't sleep until the sidewalks are shoveled and salted, the cars dug out, and the snow shaken from the low-hanging branches. I get to watch the winter from the comfort of my room. I am only outside for the twenty feet it takes to go from the car to the building when I arrive and when I leave. But now, for the second time in my desert-dwelling adult life, winter weather is keeping me from doing what I want to do when I want to do it. I push the polar vortex from my mind and meet my group for our third session.

This year's writing retreat holds twenty-five hearts and souls. We're in a newly renovated room on the ground floor called—ironically, given the weather—the Sunrise Room, sitting on black BackJacks, hunched over notebooks, socked feet wrapped warmly in yoga blankets. I'm watching them—this beautiful group of writing warriors— inhale deeply and dive into the activity I've presented. This is an evening program on our second day. They are getting tired. Writing is indeed the hard work they've heard it is. It doesn't help that this is the exercise where I ask them to name all the fears they have around their writing—their actual work, their process, their writing futures.

My legs are crossed, ankles resting on a cushion. My stuffed green monkey, Keezel, who attends all my live events to serve as a mini-Hanuman and a source of play and lightness when things get too heavy, sits on his own black cushion, holding the obligatory banana from the morning's breakfast, also watching. His stitched-on smile never wavers.

I engage in a lot of group observation when I teach. One of my biggest responsibilities is to hold the space for the group so the members can travel where their writing needs to take them. If I tune out or do my own writing, I'll lose them. I won't notice the slip of a warm tear from the lady in the corner or the unconscious clenching and unclenching of fists from the man in Padmasana (Full Lotus Pose). It's my job to notice because what I see shows me what to do next. I can't miss the signs or, worse, predetermine what the signs are supposed to be. Transformational teaching happens by remaining in the direct experience of the group. Transformational writing happens by remaining with the direct experience of the page.

The wind howls. It's evening, so the floor-to-ceiling windows are black. Anything can be out there lurking in the shadows. In the early dawn, the mountains will be laced with gray, and icicles five stories tall will suspend from the roof. Snowplows will make their endless loops through the parking lot, and we will hear the slapping of salt on the walkways. But now, all we see is pitch. All we hear is ice hitting the triple-paned glass.

I've just given my "Preach it, sister!" talk on why writing matters and why we have to cultivate the conditions necessary for our stories to grow. From that cheerleading moment, we drop straight into the dark. Into the fears that stop them in their tracks. The things that keep them from getting to the page and the things that freeze them once they get there. Our room, once spacious with optimism and hope, shrinks as the fears gain traction. Pens fly across paper. Jaws clench. It's 8:45 P.M. Poor planning on my part. We are not going to be able to finish until the next day. I almost stop them so we can do a clean closing, but my intuition holds me back. "Let them keep writing," it whispers. "The timing is perfect."

Brows furrow. Shoulders tighten. Breathing grows shallow. Tension builds, and we have not yet shared a word with one another. I tap the singing bowl to signal the end of the writing period. When the vibration stops, I ask them to share their fears. I write them on a flip chart. I have to turn the page twice. I can't write fast enough. Voices rise. Pitches increase. Fears feed on fears until the whole room pulses with them. My beautiful writers stoke the fears' fires with myths of solidarity and affirmation.

> *"Yes! Oh, yes! No one's reading! There's no point to this."*
> *"Right! I'll always be broke! My day job is what I must do."*
> *"My mother told me I couldn't do it, so I can't."*
> *"I can't write this now. What if my kids read it?"*
> *"This is just a waste of my time."*

The fears pat themselves on the shoulders. Job well done. The volume escalates until all the breath leaves the room.

"Stop," I say. "Look at what's happening. We are spinning ourselves away." We take a deep inhalation and exhalation. We shake out our arms and wrists and fingers. We stretch our jaws open. Their eyes are wide, afraid, perfectly vulnerable. I know this is the right place to stop tonight's class. And I also know they're not going to like it.

We'll meet again the next morning, but now they have to leave, unsettled and unmoored. Kripalu is a sturdy container. It will hold them until we can transform the energy. They don't believe me when I say it will be all right. They want the rah-rah motivational-speech part back. But we don't get stuck midcheer. We get stuck right here, in the dark, in the cold, on the razor's edge of dusk and dawn. We have to feel what that blade feels like so we won't turn back so quickly when we meet this place again. We have to know we won't bleed out.

The room empties. I sit with all their wildly flapping fears until they stop moving and hang in the corners of the room like bats. The bats, at least, will sleep well. They are only offering what fear ultimately gives: a message of profound importance to its intended recipient. Though all of these brave writers' fears are similar in nature, they are uniquely meaningful to each individual writer. And what these writers don't yet see is that the fears are connected to a hope—a deep yearning and desire. Fear walks hand in hand with hope, all too often causing the writer to freeze in his or her tracks, unsure which message to believe because both are so powerful, so strong. I say good night to the sleeping bats and turn out the light, knowing many of my students are still spinning, still frozen under their stiff sheets.

I walk through the quiet halls to the computer to print my boarding pass. So far, so good. Thirty minutes after returning to my room, the airline texts me the flight cancellation. I look up Chicago Midway on my phone. Red. No change. Nothing in. Nothing out. I search for Phoenix Sky Harbor Airport, even though I know it'll be open. It's always open. Yep. Status: green. My destination west across three time zones shimmers, sunny and unobstructed, waiting for me. I can see it. I know it's there. But I can't reach it. The only way home, at least on my budget, is through Chicago, which is blocked and backed up, full of discomfort and struggle.

It's after 11 P.M., and now I'm wide awake. I have to meet my class at 8:30 in the morning, but all I'm thinking is that I have to get on that plane. I'm also a full-time professor, and my semester begins next week. My college likes it when we're there for our classes. Although the irony of being trapped in the middle of my trip while I have placed my students squarely in the middle of their journeys doesn't escape me, I can't quiet my mind. I'm presenting at a world-renowned spiritual center, and I am not at all at ease with what is. I turn on the lights, slip on my shoes, and walk back to the computer. I have to climb the staircase with the gorgeous silver sign with Patanjali's wisdom in bold letters: "Yoga is seeing life as it is." Whatever.

Bleary-eyed, I log back on to the staff computer and start searching for flights. Yes! There's one! It takes thirty-two hours to get from Albany to Phoenix, going through Boston, Philadelphia, Atlanta, Minneapolis, and Los Angeles before finally landing in Arizona. I actually consider it. Only one seat left at this price! The price? $4,029. (Yes, you read that right.) I actually consider it.

It's inching toward midnight. I place a call to my college dean, knowing this is the equivalent of drunk-calling an ex-lover. My voice is low and tired. "Hey," I say to her voicemail. "It's Laraine, and I can't get home." I leave a rambling message for her until the machine disconnects me.

The distraction of calling my dean prevents the knee-jerk reaction of buying a $4,000 plane ticket. I can't stay here. For once, I did not overpack. I have the minimum amount of toiletries, clothing, and contraband Starbucks individual coffee packets. I didn't even bring my computer.

I return to the airline website. It's still holiday travel time. It's hard to get a flight when everything is working. I'd bought these tickets in July. I click forward one more day. No flights available. Two more days. None. Three more days. The first flight I can bump to is five days out. Well. Click.

The group is subdued when we meet the next morning. Angry, even, at being left so vulnerable. I am tired. Patanjali is still on my nerves. The windows are steel gray this morning. The frozen bushes that line the exterior walls shiver.

It would have been easier if I had skipped this part—this treacherous off-road trek that triggered their emotions. It's easier to present a call-to-action workshop. Easier to rally people, pump them up, and then slip quickly away while their endorphins are still pumping. Likewise, it's easier for writers to start a lot of projects and make quick course adjustments when they feel uncomfortable. But we don't move forward by perpetually starting over. Sometimes, we just have to wait. We have to feel the itch and resist the urge to scratch. Even Keezel, my trusted monkey mascot, can't make them laugh that bitter morning. He did his classic backflip routine. Nothing.

These writers are so brave, but they don't see it yet. They are uncomfortable, but they are here. They have returned to our classroom. They did not sleep in. They did not stay away. Kripalu's thick walls and the unprecedented subzero temperatures held them close. And apparently, the polar vortex isn't letting me go anytime soon either.

We sit in silence for a bit, shoulders and jaws and throats and hearts softening with the gift of breath. The bats flutter, unfurl their wings, and—more quietly this time—fly to their writer of choice and perch on their shoulders. When the bats still and the group surrenders, we begin the real work of the retreat.

Inspiration without action is short-lived. The middle, even when it feels frozen and immutable, is always in motion. Things align and release beneath the surface that can only become visible with time and attention. If we rush a thaw, we risk a mudslide. A flood. A washing away of what we want to keep as well as what we want to let go.

At last, they pick up their pens and begin to question everything. They breathe. One by one, the bats whisper their responses. One by one, the bats transform into new creations—new ideas, thoughts, and forms. The room itself exhales. The writing speed picks up. Kleenex makes the rounds. The fears are speaking their precise messages that resonate only with their intended writer—their *beloved.*

Outside it is still deadly cold, but underneath the roof of this ancient monastery, we are melting into motion, dancing with the grinning green monkey to Prince's "Let's Go Crazy." Inside, we are transforming.

I don't get home for six more days. I have to write by hand again since I have no personal computer. I wander the bookstore. I try on expensive yoga clothes, then hang them back up. I ration my Starbucks packets. I can do nothing but wait. Nothing but inquire into what surfaces in the dark; remember my courageous students; and trust in the gifts and surprises that always come with the exhalation of surrender, an opening heart, and a crisp, blank page. One of those gifts?

You guessed it. This book.

Introduction

Hear this: The block that you (and all creatives) experience at various times during your work is natural, normal, and part of the whole deal. Nothing is wrong with you. This is part of being an artist. Getting stuck is necessary. But it turns out getting stuck isn't the problem. The meaning you make out of getting stuck is the issue. We must revise the meaning we make of this natural part of the process.

You aren't doing anything wrong when you find yourself stumped. You aren't doing anything millions haven't done before when you turn away from your book—unsure, afraid, maybe even a little angry at it for somehow letting you down. Sometimes, the writing process feels so overwhelming, we just throw up our hands and stop. When we don't know what a good next step is, or what the right next step is, it's easy to panic and freeze, exacerbating the intensity of the natural pause in the creative process. Don't turn away. Things are just about to get interesting.

I don't believe in writer's block, per se, but I know very well the feeling of suddenly being stuck in my writing. The difference for me is that I don't see writer's block as the wolf at the door or the obstacle to be destroyed, mowed down, squelched. Instead, I see it as a pause. A signal to pay attention to something. I can't tell you what that something is for you, but I can share with you ways of finding out. Writer's block is a signpost that alerts you to where you're going. It forces you to slow down, to put the brakes on so you won't barrel forward, unthinking and unaware, into the next thing. It prevents you from publishing too quickly—pressing Send too fast. It is a safety belt, keeping you from crashing through the windshield.

The process you'll find in this book is integrative. It won't minimize your experience or provide pithy solutions. My approach teaches connection and dialogue. It focuses on inquiry, within both yourself and your work to keep yourself on track. And it's rooted in the understanding that you are in a relationship with your writing and with the work itself. Like all relationships, there are changes of plans. Diversions and miscommunications. Fights, even. But with the relationships that matter, there's an eventual circling back together. A coming home to each other, stronger for having navigated the uncharted course.

Instead of reacting to the block, I encourage you to stop and look at it. Listen to it. Touch it. Find out what its gifts are, what it's offering you. This block—this pause—emerged from you and your work. It is a part of that work, just as much as your characters are. Before you get out the ax, pour it some tea. Have a conversation. You may find you can hold hands across the table instead. You may find the block itself is the very heart of your work.

Using Inquiry to Work through Blocks

In this book, I share a Deep Inquiry Path for writer's block. We will use questioning to deepen our relationship to our writing and our blocks. We are seeking a more sophisticated understanding of our work and process, and from that new place of awareness, we will see windows where we once saw only walls. In the Deep Inquiry Path, we will not force a predetermined answer from ourselves or our work. Instead we will cultivate an essential, sacred relationship with our work and seek a deeper understanding of what our work is offering us. Inquiry is a powerful tool for exploring the nature of what we feel is blocked and for helping both our work and us as writers to move forward. We have to grow so our work can grow.

As writers, we're probably more than accustomed to the periods of seemingly endless vacant window staring that accompany the writing process. We may have heard or otherwise internalized comments from others that characterize our writing as wasting time. To some people, what we're doing may have no perceived value if there is no product. Writers tend to have temperaments and dispositions that allow us to remain alone in a room as long as it takes to bring back the fruits of our labors. We're OK with being by ourselves. In fact, we thrive in the company of the page and the characters in our heads and hearts. This ability to be alone and look inward is a fantastic skill set to use to move through blocks. We are perfectly positioned to use the tools we can already access to deepen our work through questioning. You may think active questioning and experimentation have more to do with the sciences—with inventors and researchers. But remember that writing is also an experimenting art, and goodness, are we ever inventors! Writing is also a science of questions.

Too often, we're taught to track only an outcome—a result. But what about pursuing our curiosity? What about following the bread crumbs we find along the way? There's not much room for that conscious wandering, this soulful meandering, in modern life, but increasingly, research is showing us the value of unstructured activity and time—the value of unregulated play, not just in children but in adults as well—and the importance of creating space for surprises. It is quite hard to be surprised if everything is planned out in advance.

You may fear that you will lose momentum if you keep questioning everything. Perhaps you're afraid you'll just get lost in the work. Won't everything just be worse? We can attach so deeply to what we think we have and where we think we're going that any deviation is a threat to the work itself. The Deep Inquiry Path that I'll show you will allow you to have these necessary diversions—these times of conscious meandering—but the questions will also keep you focused on the work at hand. You won't have to worry about not finding your way back. You'll have left your own bread crumbs along the way.

This book offers lots of different kinds of activities to help you deepen your relationship with your writing and move you forward when you feel unsure of the next step. They won't all work for you. Some that are effective today won't work tomorrow. That's the shape-shifting nature of practice. That's the dance we do with our work. We grow the relationship slowly, and our breakthrough moments arise from that steady pace. The Deep Inquiry questions, which are the heart of this book, can be applied in as many ways as you can imagine to your stories and your process. Please don't be afraid to listen to your inner wisdom. All of the activities in the book are doors. Where you go when you step through them is entirely your journey to make.

To that end, I encourage you to create your own Foundation Tool Kit. This kit will consist of practices, prompts, movement activities, playlists—anything you can think of that will help you move forward and deeper into your work. These tools will be your tried-and-true touchstones, your allies in your process. You can think of them as micropractices, things you can do in just a few minutes to realign yourself, stop the free fall into fight-or-flight responses, and break unhelpful thought patterns.

Before we dive in, remember these points:

» Writing is a slow process. It is not typing. It is a synthesis of past, present, and future. It's the condensation of an idea, a vision, or an experience into a focused sensory experience on the page. It's the deepest form of sharing—one imagination to another. It's the most intimate form of communication—mind to mind, heart to heart. This synthesis does not happen in one sitting, one week, one month, or one year. It happens slowly over months and years of paying deeper and deeper attention to your process and the fruits that come from that work.

» It takes many drafts and lots of revision to get to a final product. Think of painting a room. The primer coat goes on first, long before the edge work gets done. Your early drafts are the primer coats. Let them be that. Avoid going back and reworking an early draft.

» Writing is worthwhile. Our work matters.

Throughout this book, you'll use questions to enhance your work and life. Think of them as living questions. They may promote more questions or prompt you to take a slightly different approach to a question. That's perfect. You don't have to accept this work exactly as it's presented. Please make the questions and activities your own. Use them flexibly and intuitively. You can modify anything to suit your circumstances. Don't be afraid to take ownership of your process. Who else will?

PART ONE **When You Meet the Block**

1 | Cultivate a Relationship with Your Writing

Our stories are waiting for us to find them. Sometimes we have to coax them out. Sometimes we have to listen beneath the chatter of what is not relevant. Our stories need us to bring them into the world. Don't forget that part. By our willingness to learn *with* our art, we can transform our readers' worlds as well. When you commit to a consistent writing practice, you're cultivating a relationship with your writing. To work through blocks, you need to be comfortable with and invested in the concept of being in this relationship. You and your writing (you can refer to it as your muse, your source, your inspiration—whatever works for you) are both sovereign beings who need each other to come to full fruition. Your writing helps you regardless of whether you publish or not, and you help your writing by providing a vehicle (pen and paper, a keyboard) for it to enter this world.

If you've neglected this relationship in the past, you have to work to prove that you're back. For real. Not just until the next shiny thing comes along. Cultivating a relationship with your writing can feel like feeding a feral cat. Have you ever tried that? Gaining the trust of a wild animal requires patience and compassion. You may want to run right up and pet the kitty, brush his fur, and wrap him up to take home. But he's not going to play along. He's in survival mode. He needs to know he can trust you. He needs to know you're in this relationship for the long haul.

Just like a feral cat, your writing is a separate being, and it has its own needs. Don't be dissuaded. Demonstrate patience and compassion. Offer it nourishment through committed practice. Don't judge the outcomes of these practice sessions. You're building trust. You're establishing connection. You're doing your part. Trust that. Sooner than you think, you'll be sharing your life with a wild and fierce companion.

As you begin cultivating a long-term approach to the creative process, try to create a harmonious relationship rather than one of discord. Better your writing be a companion and trusted friend than a critic or a moody adversary. Remember that you and your writing are not adversaries, you're not at cross-purposes, and you're not here to sabotage one another. When we view ourselves in relationship to our writing, it's easier to make and keep our commitments to it. We become less attached to a single encounter. We begin to consider how we and our writing can serve each other and, by doing that, develop goodwill and trust.

Your writing is out there waiting, whether you are currently talking with it or not. Sure, you can walk away from it from time to time. Maybe even years. You can leave the room, but you get called back. There's a writing-size hole in your life, a nagging feeling that you've left something important behind. Characters and stories follow you around, whispering to you in the dark, haunting you. Most of us know what it feels like to be haunted by what we're not writing. That haunting is simply the call of our writing asking us to come back. You and your writing were meant for each other. Reach out your hand.

Our talents transform into the tools we need to help us love and live more deeply. Writing is one of our gifts. When we use it, we expand and grow. When we ignore or neglect it, we suffer. Our gifts need to be used so they can fully manifest. You've been given the gift of writing because it will be beneficial for all aspects of your life, not just your writing life. It's part of what makes you, you. It's like a physical system. Your writing is as integral to your existence as your circulatory system. It's embedded in your cells. Ignite a relationship with that potential and you'll be unstoppable. This requires nurture, commitment, persistence, discipline, patience, and a profound trust. You do your part, and your writing will do its part. When you try to do all the lifting, you collapse. Work together, each of you carrying the part of the load that is yours.

Your writing is your companion for life. You came into the world with it, and it will be with you until the end. So rise up and meet it. Create a sustainable relationship with your writing that's based on mutual respect, trust, and commitment. You are not your writing, and your writing is not you. Both of you are sovereign beings. Your writing, however, needs you to carry what it has to offer into the world. It cannot pick up a pen or type on a computer and share a story. It needs you for that. Your writing knocks at the door of your heart and invites you to pick up your pen. Won't you answer?

DEEP INQUIRY PRACTICE

Meeting the Inner Writer Meditation

This meditation invites you to create a space where you and your writing can find each other. We'll build on this idea in subsequent chapters when we discuss the Storyverse. Envisioning yourself and your writing in relationship to each other creates a greater sense of ease and communion between you, and it also helps you cultivate active imagination, a necessary component of the writing process.

This meditation helps you practice getting out of your own way so you can access active imagination more easily. Counterintuitively, the most direct approach to solve a problem is sometimes the least effective. You can discover much of the magic of writing by meandering and exploring in ways that may seem at first to lack focus or purpose.

If possible, shut the door to your writing space and close your eyes. Sit comfortably either in a chair or on the floor. The important thing is to be comfortable. If you're in a chair, ground your feet on the floor. If you're sitting on the floor already, let the bowl of your hips sink into the ground beneath you, your hands resting on your lap or your knees. Bring your attention to your breath. Take a deep inhalation followed by a deep exhalation. Relax your jaw. Your tongue. The back of your throat. Bring your shoulders up to your ears and then release them. You might want to release with sound. Settle yourself into your body and your breath.

Now you're going to journey into your heart, into the dwelling place of writing. Begin by conjuring the room where your writing lives. This can be an internal structure or an external landscape. It can be a mountain range. Perhaps it's beside an ocean. In a living room or a coffee shop. On a bus. It can be a combination of all those things. It doesn't matter what you see. Simply pay attention to what you're observing, because this is the space where clues are going to surface that will help guide you into a more meaningful relationship with your writing.

Helpful hint: You can't do this wrong.

Pause and imagine. What does the space that houses your writing look like? Notice the textures and colors. Do you hear any sounds? Do you notice any smells? What is the temperature? What do you see? Are there windows? If you're outside, what is the sky like? What about the weather pattern? Take some time here to explore your inner vision, and to observe, touch, and smell this world where your writing lives. Make some notes in your journal. Be as specific as you can be. You may want to have an audio recorder (your smartphone works!) nearby to describe what you're observing, so you don't have to break the moment to write.

When you feel ready to move on, step deeper into the room or landscape. What is the very first thing, object, or animal you notice? Walk up to this item and begin to examine it. What do you observe? What's the shape? Is it warm? Cool? Is it spiky? Smooth?

When you're ready, if you'd like to take this object or companion with you, ask it for permission to do so before you disturb its place. Don't disturb it if it doesn't wish to move.

As you continue deeper into the space, either with your new companion or alone, begin to notice again how the room or space appears around you. Has anything shifted? Light to dark? Dark to light? Warm to cold? Cool to warm? Neutral to color?

When you feel fully present in this space, ask your writing if it will appear for you. Your writing might be an actual person. It might appear like an animal or a symbol or a ball of energy. It might be a word. It doesn't matter what it looks like. Just ask it to please make itself known. What do you observe here? What are the qualities of your writing? How do you feel to be in the same space with it? How do you think it feels to be in the same space with you?

Remember to breathe. Pay attention to the way your breath is moving in your body. A deep, full inhalation and exhalation helps to create space and softness.

If you haven't already done so, move closer to your writing. Notice what occurs. How does that movement feel? Do you want to get even closer? Do you feel fearful? Do you feel an attraction or a repulsion toward moving closer to your writing? We're just observing, not judging. Maybe you're meeting each other for the first time. It's like a first date, and you're both a little awkward. Or maybe it feels like you've reconnected with a lifelong friend. You can pick up right where you left off.

In your journal, write on these three prompts:

1. Begin by introducing yourself to your writing and sharing a little bit of your hopes, dreams, and ideas for how the two of you can work together.
2. Enter into a dialogue with your writing, beginning with a question: What does your writing need from you in order to be as full and deep and rich as it is capable of being? In other words, what can you give your writing to help it reach its fullest potential?
3. Reverse roles. This time, your writing is asking you what it can do to help you reach your fullest and deepest potential. Take time to listen for the answer that emerges.

When you feel complete with this time with your writing, ask it one more question: What is the one most important thing that needs to happen now so that the two of you can work more harmoniously? Write it down. Trust your first response—your intuition. You don't have to know how it's going to work. You don't have to have a plan. You're just listening and trusting at this point.

When you feel complete with this, thank your writing. Take in the landscape where your writing lives. Now that you know what this room or this landscape is like, and you know what your writing feels like, you can visit this place at any time. You can always return to your writing and ask it questions. When you're trying to envision the world of your story, ask your writing what's the next thing you need to do. Let it help you. You don't have to figure it out ahead of time.

Offer gratitude to your writing for having appeared when you requested and offer gratitude to yourself for appearing when requested, and as you leave the room or landscape, take note of anything that might have shifted or changed, understanding that the space where your writing lives may look different every time you access it. It's not stagnant. Your writing and its world, just like you and your world, are always in motion.

When you're ready to come back to our world, take some deep breaths—full inhalations and full exhalations. Slowly open your eyes, keeping your gaze soft and focused inward, and slowly come to standing. Shake out your fingers, wrists, arms, and shoulders. Raise your arms over your head and slowly bend forward if you can, hands moving toward the earth, touching the ground if that's possible. Pause for three full breaths. Slowly, slowly return to standing, with your head the last to come up.

2 | Learn to Move through the World as a Writer

Nothing stays the same. The fantastic writing practice you had yesterday will be different today, and different yet again tomorrow. Some of our practices make us feel invincible. Others less so. Don't forget that you hold the results of perseverance, patience, discipline, and faith when you read a book. You hold the changes the author had to move through in order to make art. You hold *transformation* in your hands. Magic. The fruition of one writer's willingness to journey into the unknown. You hold bravery. Hope. Relentless curiosity. These are traits of the writer who finishes projects. The writer who creates stories and poems that matter. The writer who never forgets that writing is part of her DNA.

You, too, value these things—the wrestling of words onto pages—or you wouldn't have picked up this book. You would have remained content with "good enough," with all the excuses the world would love to sell you to keep you silent: *No one's reading anymore. You'll never make any money. Who do you think you are? You don't have any talent anyway.* You would have let those voices win. But you did not.

There will always be those sounds, those background noises. Those who want to turn you away from your work. But their cries are about them, not you. You know there's another side to this coin, and more important, you know you can get there.

Being a writer is not about the number of books you have written on your shelves. Being a writer is a way of navigating the world. A way of seeing, listening, feeling, and imagining all that is around you. A writer is never *not* a writer, whether a pen or computer is on hand or not. Everything we do in a day feeds our lives as writers. Dissolve the false separation of "when I am writing" and "when I am not writing." Writers are always writers. We're always engaged with all the elements that enable us to be creative on the page. Our lives aren't separated from those sensibilities, those gifts. Learning to move through the world *as* a writer—as opposed to trying to meet the impossible idea of *being* a writer—will help you create a realistic, beneficial relationship with your work.

Train yourself to deepen your observational skills. Train your writer's ear to pick up the sounds of story that surround you all the time. You can do all your daily activities—work, laundry, grocery shopping, driving—and find all the elements of your chosen art within them. I invite you to broaden and deepen your definition of being a writer. As you realize that every breath you take holds the potential for a story, you will begin moving into an integrative relationship with your writing—a companionship, a friendship—each holding the other up as you walk together through life as partners and cocreators.

You can claim your power as a writer by engaging in the world *as a writer* and teaching yourself how to gather your material. Having your own resources to draw from when you're blocked serves two primary purposes. First, it reinforces an awareness that you always have what you need within you. It cultivates inner trust. You don't have to attend an expensive workshop or buy another book (though there's nothing wrong with doing either of these things) when you get stuck. You've already gathered a wealth of things from which to choose ideas. Second, gathering material helps train you to move through the world as a writer. It teaches you to pay attention. Any and every place you go is an opportunity to collect impressions, whether it's a scent, a forgotten memory, a trinket from a thrift shop, or the view of a sunset from the seaside. In your day-to-day experience, what strikes you as interesting? What do you wonder about? What do you question? What reminds you of something you can't quite touch?

Writers are profoundly observant. We are always paying attention to what's around us, what's underneath and what's above. With practice, we realize that though we may not know why we're drawn to something, the reason will eventually reveal itself. We move through the world with all five senses and our precious intuition engaged. Every step forward contains the possibility for everything that comes after.

Getting Stuck Is Also Part of Writing

The creative process has natural ebbs and flows. When you find your writing in an ebb tide, do what writers do: keep showing up no matter what the outcome (or lack thereof).

If you expect every day to be flush with productivity, you're setting yourself up for disappointment. Though the way through a writing block is writing, misguided advice like "just write" can have a minimizing and shaming effect on a writer. Nike's Just Do It campaign was a brilliant slogan, but if it were truly that easy for people to exercise, there'd be no need for spin classes. We all have methods for getting in our own way. It's human nature. And whereas I don't think there is any great conspiracy at work to block our writing, I do think there are myriad ways we trip ourselves up without realizing it. When we can't see the particular ocean we're swimming in, advice to just get out of the water (that we don't even see) is not at all helpful.

If you're stuck, be stuck. Name it. Own it. Once you can name it, you can reframe your relationship with it. In other words, you can shift the meaning of being stuck. When things remain amorphous, they easily become overwhelming. You can't address what you can't define. When you dismiss or invalidate your own experience, you forfeit the opportunity to learn from that experience. You can't explore and shift that which you deny exists.

So many of us are well trained to minimize our feelings: "No, I'm not angry"; "No, I'm not sad. I'm fine." Minimization and denial of our direct experiences don't serve us as writers, nor do they serve our writing. Writers who can't remain in their own direct experience can't bring that presence—so essential to storytelling—to the page.

Be fully *in* your experience, knowing it is impermanent. You can't reach the door to the other side if you don't claim your current position. The first step to releasing the energy your writer's block holds is to acknowledge that something is holding that energy. Sounds obvious, right? But you can't do that if you're diminishing or denying what you're currently feeling. The time for pretending is over. Be real with yourself. Then you can be real on the page.

DEEP INQUIRY PRACTICES

Writer's Drawer

Remember the days of card catalogs at the library? Maybe you're too young to have pulled out one of those rickety drawers by its brass handle, a yellowed typed label indicating what you might find in its narrow trunk. The cards themselves were smudged, folded, dotted with light pencil etchings. More knowledge, more questions, and more stories than a human being could hope to read in a dozen lifetimes were contained within that single drawer. And that was just one drawer! We seekers had a tangible item to hold that showed us, whether we liked it or not, that there was more to this world than we would ever know. The card catalog, with its thick legs and solid middle, gave us the gift of humility. Other writers, scholars, scientists, and poets have been where we are now, have contributed to the larger conversation, and have passed on to other realms.

The card catalog—much more powerful than our online instant access to everything ever published because we can actually see it, touch it, and marvel at it—never let us forget that we were individuals among many. When we do an online search, we may be able to find everything, but we only see what fits on our screen. We can't hold the heft of the work online. When we hold a single drawer from a card catalog, we feel the weight of ideas in our palms. It registers in our bodies. Digital data weigh nothing. It's harder for us to feel this information's power. It's easier for us to dismiss it.

Consider creating your own card catalog for your life as a writer. A writer's drawer (literal or metaphorical, virtual or analog) contains the things you've gathered, imagined, read about, listened to, hoped for, and created for your writing life. It's a place you can visit to find character ideas. To grab a snippet of dialogue to get you started. To find intriguing textures for your settings. To ultimately remind yourself that yes, you are a writer, and you have moved through your life as one. You have been paying attention, and even when things didn't seem to be working as you thought they should, they were still working.

A writer's drawer helps you remember that sometimes the greatest progress occurs when it seems like nothing is happening. Being a writer is a way of being in the world—a way of relating to the people and things with which we come in contact. We don't turn it on and off based on whether or not we're sitting at a desk.

Who's in your drawer? When you pull out your card you won't have to stare at a blank page. You'll have a place to begin. Even if what you've gathered is only the doorway into where you need to go, what a valuable gift you will have given yourself.

Writer's Word Bag

Begin keeping a word bag. The phenomenal cartoonist, teacher, and writer Lynda Barry encourages her students to keep word bags. These bags can contain any word you gather throughout your day: single words, phrases, sounds, textures, smells, tastes, experiences. You can keep them on your smartphone, record them in an old-fashioned notebook, or even write them on slips of paper and place them in an actual bag. You don't have to know why you're selecting the words. You don't have to know where or if they'll fit. You are just creating a nonlinear word record of your day.

This word bag will be a source of inspiration throughout your writing life. You can pull items from the bag to create random writing prompts. By accumulating the words for your bag, you will start to notice synchronicities and patterns. You'll also cultivate a deeper presence in your daily life and train your writer's eye and ear.

3 | Create a Consistent Practice

Psychologists have long been fascinated with the concepts of creativity and genius. Although researchers can't yet tease apart whether the desire to master something yields greater achievement or whether having innate talent creates that greater desire for mastery, it's indisputable that practice creates *something*. You've likely heard of the ten thousand hours concept made famous by Malcolm Gladwell in *The Tipping Point*. The theory states that it takes approximately ten thousand hours of practice at something before you can begin to see significant improvement. Whether it's ten thousand hours or a hundred thousand hours, there's no doubt that the more you show up, the better you'll be.

Writing, like any creative process, is an endurance sport. It's a long game. You may experience short bursts of inspiration, but if you're a serious player, you know some days won't go according to plan. You know that's part of the process. Athletes practice. Musicians practice. Writers practice too; that's what drafting is. That's what writing exercises are. Our practice includes the "sketches" that don't quite come together—the free throws that don't swoosh through the basket. But we're not bothered by that. We keep going because—say it with me—that's what serious artists do.

As you build your creative practice, you'll soon start to see the fruition that comes from consistency. Without having set rigid goals, you've nonetheless created some work. This always happens. Showing up for your writing creates writing, which, over time, yields a body of work.

The more consistent you are, the more you'll observe that no day is the same. A great session one day doesn't guarantee a great session the next day. You'll learn to roll with it. You've set your practice in motion, and you're on your way. A day that offers only a few words is just one day that offered only a few words. Don't make it mean any more than that. The next session will be different. Show up. Move along. This practice is a continuum. One day's events, whether you view them as successful or unsuccessful, are only one day's events. They don't mean anything. What matters is your commitment to the marathon.

Build Up Your Momentum

The word *momentum* is derived from the Latin verb *movere,* meaning "to move." It can take a lot of force to start pushing a rock forward, but as it builds up speed, it doesn't need as much of your energy to keep it moving. In your writing practice, consistency builds momentum. Whether you're writing for fifteen minutes three days a week, two hours four days a week, or some other combination, the more you maintain your consistency, the greater the momentum you'll build up.

By maintaining a consistent practice, you'll reap these gifts of momentum:

» You'll gain insight into how you feel on days you write versus days you don't.
» You'll gain an acceptance of a variety of creative outputs on different days.
» You'll learn to detach from a particular day's session, relieving yourself of stress and anxiety over your writing.
» You'll learn, through direct experience, that what you devote time and energy to will subsequently grow and deepen.
» You'll find that there are macro and micro levels to a writing session. The macro level is the book itself—your larger work. The micro level is what is happening word by word on the page in front of you.

Never underestimate the power of consistent practice. If you write only when you feel inspired and excited to do it, you'll be a sporadic writer. You'll grow dependent on the idea of inspiration as the required motivator for your writing, and you'll predetermine whether or not it's a good day to write without writing a thing. Inspiration is the companion of practice. The more consistent your practice, the more inspired you'll become.

DEEP INQUIRY PRACTICES

Become Aware of How You Use Your Time

Record your time usage during a typical week. Understand that no week unfolds in exactly the same way, but use a week where you're not on vacation or nursing a sick relative or working an unusual amount of overtime. Keep track of everything—from time preparing food to time getting dressed, driving to work, watching television, surfing the Internet, visiting with friends, your job commitments, and yes, your writing. Before you can create a reasonable writing schedule, you first have to know how you currently allocate your time.

Remember to use nonjudgment here. If you learn you're spending twenty-five hours a week on Facebook, that's valuable to know. If that works for you, no problem. If it doesn't, then you have a starting point to begin shifting your time usage. Until you know what you're currently doing with your time, you have no baseline to create changes. As Carl Sandburg tells us, "Time is the coin of your life. Be careful, lest others spend it for you." We need to know how we are spending our minutes. They are more precious to a writer than dollars.

After you have your "typical" week's schedule, take a look at it and evaluate where you can *consistently* create time for your writing. You don't have to write every day to create an effective and fulfilling practice, but you do have to show up regularly. Find three times a week. Four perhaps. Find thirty minutes during a weekday. Find an extra hour on the weekend. You choose the amount and location of that writing time and give it a whirl. Don't pretend that you don't have to go to work from eight to five, Monday through Friday, if you do. Work with what you have and where you are. Bring writing *into the life you have* rather than attempting to create a different life that you think will be better suited to writing. Bring writing in *now*. Create a schedule for the next week and see what happens. Record your time usage again. Evaluate, adjust, and move forward.

The powersheets in the appendix will help you evolve a writing practice. On powersheet 1, fill in your planned schedule for the next seven days. Note as well where you intend to show up for your writing. Then, on powersheet 2, record what actually happens. Evaluate, adjust, and move forward to the next week. Do not fill out all forty-nine days at once but proceed in seven-day increments. Moving more slowly and with greater awareness will help you create more effective, lasting changes. Remember to be flexible. No one is telling you that you must write eight hours a day, seven days a week, to "be" a writer. You determine the time blocks that work for you—for what you want to accomplish with your work *and* for how much communion with your writing you need for your emotional well-being. The powersheets help you establish sovereign creative boundaries within which you and your work can connect.

Inner Journal Questions

Observe yourself with soft eyes as you nurture your practice. Consider these questions in your journal:

- » What enhances and fuels my practice?
- » What depletes my energy?
- » What differences do I see between an endurance sport and a short game? What insights can I apply to my creative process?
- » What activities will best prepare me for a writer's long game?
- » What subtle differences in how I relate to my writing do I notice day to day?
- » What larger differences do I notice over time?
- » What gifts do I receive from my flexible yet consistent practice?

4 | Understand the Type of Block You're Working With

Because writing and the writing process have so many different layers and levels, it can help to have a framework through which to view different kinds of blocks. I have broken writer's block down into two primary categories: writer-in-process blocks and work-in-progress blocks.

Writer-in-Process

Writer-in-process blocks occur when you are working on your book, and the book is requiring you to face parts of yourself or your beliefs about the book that you'd rather not acknowledge. They may relate to what you believe being a writer is or isn't or how you feel others may respond to your work. They may be fears, patterns of behavior (such as procrastination or perfectionism), or unresolved personal issues.

Think back to the last book you read and resonated with. How did you come to find that book? Did a friend recommend it to you? Were you drawn to the cover? A blurb on the back? The author? A review? There's often something a bit magical and synchronous about finding a book. We can't "force-find" a book any more than we can force-find a best friend or a spouse. Some would say the book chooses us. We enter a bookstore, perhaps on a mission to find a specific thing. But we wander, as is necessary in bookstores. We have a quick look around and make initial judgments: yes, no, maybe, my type, not my type. Some of these choices are rational and conscious. Others are intuitive. "Will you take me home with you?" Yes. No. Maybe. Then the big unknown: When we get home, will it work out?

While most people who enjoy reading can derive pleasure from many kinds of books, even if they don't all spark the heart, the reasons we carry a book in our hearts as opposed to our heads are far more mysterious. What makes us fall in love with one book and not another? It's less about writing style than about the way the story and characters shifted something in our hearts. As Lisa Cron tells us in her book *Wired for Story*, "Even the most lyrical, beautiful writing by itself is as inviting as a big bowl of waxed fruit." In other words, a perfectly written still life is only a still life. We are moved by a book when we viscerally connect to and are transformed by the journey of the characters. How are we changed by the struggles the characters go through, and how are those challenges relevant to our lives?

To better understand writer-in-process blocks, let's examine the writer-book-reader trifecta. A text itself is neutral. It is only words—marks on a page—until the reader cracks the spine. The reader makes the neutral text come alive. No reader has the same connection to any text, because the words of that neutral text are filtered through each reader's lens of the world. Story lines and characters that have particular emotional charges—either positive or negative—are unique to each reader, less because of the literal story on the page than because of the meaning and relevance the reader makes of the events of the story. The story triggers something of emotional significance (or not), and the reader makes associations with the story that are personally significant. No writer can predict how this connection or disconnection will unfold.

For this amazing magic and alchemy to occur, writers have to have a unique journey of transformation with the text. We must go forth into the dark (or the blinding white of the page) and gather what is there to be brought back. We cannot finish a book at the same level of consciousness at which we began it. We evolve because we experience—vicariously perhaps, but certainly viscerally—the suffering and turmoil of our characters as we write their stories. We are cocreators on their narrative journey. We can't avoid where our story is taking us. If we do, we won't be able to take our readers there, and no one will connect with our work at all. We are not our characters, but we are walking with them on their path. We must be connected to the questions and struggles of our characters somehow, or we could not sustain the curiosity and momentum to finish the book. This call toward our own transformation as authors can cause us to feel blocked. Our work is requiring us to become the writer who can write the book. That's big, brave work.

Our curiosity and wonder about our own work is connected to its personal pull with our own evolution. This unfolding and evolution occurs differently with each book we write, because each of our books is linked with a different aspect of our own growth. We must be willing to go to the front lines first—to face the demands of the narrative, of the craft, of solitude—and be willing to knowingly subject ourselves to change in order to create a text that, though it means something deep and personal to us as writers, must then go on to be a commodity—a good traded in the marketplace for currency. A writer-in-process is a writer in the natural state of psychological, spiritual, and emotional evolution required to do the work she is called to do.

A book is never neutral to its writer, yet it becomes neutral when it enters the market, and only when a reader finds it and wakes it up does it no longer hold neutrality. When that happens, when the reader touches the book, the trifecta is complete. The work has found a home. The writer's evolution supported the character's evolution, which in turn supported the reader's evolution. There's not much more sacred on this earth than that.

Can you see how much our work matters? How essential it is that we take the time to cultivate our gifts? To show up regularly and bring forth our part of the bargain? Don't doubt your value as a writer for a second. A reader is waiting for you to be brave enough to go first.

Let's review. First, you show up and do your work. Second, you release that work into the world to do its job. Third, the reader holds the effort, wakes it up by reading, and sparks magic. You're joined together—three beings for a single, magic moment—as one.

Remember that your book—your writing—pulls you forward. It is asking you to be the writer who can write it. It's asking you to be willing to grow and change enough to be the one who can write what you are being called to write. To do that, you're going to be faced with all the things swimming around inside that may trigger writer-in-process blocks. Don't be afraid to let them loose. Don't be afraid of what you might find. The heart of your story lives there.

Work-in-Progress Blocks

I have never been able to learn how to drive a car with a standard transmission. Many brave people have tried to teach me—in their own cars, no less—but to no avail. I understood what to do. I memorized the order of the gears and which foot is supposed to do what. But because I have been driving with an automatic transmission since 1984, I have no idea what to do when forced to relate to gears in a different way. An empty parking lot terrifies me. I'll start moving forward and then have to make a decision. Where do I put that foot? What the heck is the clutch supposed to do again? Why is that necessary? Crap. I forgot to look in any mirrors because I have been so worried about my feet. Now the car is making this horrific noise. My noble teacher and car's owner is gripping the door handle, trying not to say what no doubt must be in his thoughts. No matter what, I can't move forward. The engine grinds and eventually stalls. I hoped so much to make it around the parking lot. But I panicked and froze, unable to do anything, and the car mirrored my paralysis.

This analogy to writer's block can show you the very real physical immobility that can occur when you're faced with the combination of heavy expectations and lack of skill. Craft holds up art. The grandest dreams for your book cannot materialize if you don't have the necessary technical knowledge. Simply put: We have to know what we're doing with our tools. We have to know how to shift the gears. Work-in-progress blocks relate to problems with the product itself. They may include issues with the structure, characters, dramatic conflict, research, and your current level of ability to complete the project as envisioned.

A work-in-progress, by its very definition, is evolving. It is showing the writer more and more about its nature with every chapter written. It is impossible to predetermine this evolution and thus avoid the craft and structural issues in a work as it's evolving. I've never worked on a book that didn't come along part and parcel with some kind of stopping point. Some kind of "Holy moly, what on earth am I doing?" moment. Some kind of resistance and self-doubt. Some kind of nasty noise in my head telling me it's all for naught.

For me, this usually falls between drafts two and three of a book. So much writing has already been done. So many hours with just my notebook, computer, and me. I'll read through it and see how far I still have to go. "But you've already spent a year on it!" that voice in my head will say. "You've invested so much already. It's good enough." And I'll begin to freeze. Find myself hanging out on Facebook for too long. Buying shoes with one-click. Deciding now would be a good time to learn Spanish or get another cat. I'll walk out to the mailbox, even though I never get any actual mail anymore except invitations to attend retirement investment seminars (no obligation!) at a steak-house or purchase some kind of hearing aid device. I'll think about how I used to get mail. How everything about a career as a writer involved the mail. I had an in-home scale once so I could stamp my submissions appropriately. Now nothing comes but coupons that move straight to the recycle bin. I'll let myself stand in that mind-circling place for a good twenty minutes before walking back inside and deciding that, well, I've had enough for today. The book is a joke anyway. I'm a joke. The world has absolutely no need of my contribution. Hello, Netflix, my greatest friend.

On and on we'll go, my thoughts and I, until I walk back upstairs to my office and get back to work. The demoralizing tone that I once applied to "Oh gosh, look at all the wasted work you've done," shifts to the affirmative approach: "Wow. Look at all that work you've done. You're a rock star." And so we move forward, my book and I. A little more world-weary. A little more aware that what we thought the book would become is not what it will be. That's always the case, you know. Your idea of the book is only the door into the book. The book itself is always so much more than you can understand at first.

You *will* encounter things as you draft that are going to show you where you need to go, which will force you to change or cut things you've already written. That's the nature of the process. The realization that something doesn't work is a gift. You can't know how to revise if you can't identify what needs work. Rather than this revelation being discouraging, it is *encouraging*. Your work is speaking to you, and because you wrote all those words in that particular order, the issue was revealed. That's an important reframe. *The pages that went before the awareness of a problem were the paths to that problem.* How cool is that? Within that problem lies the key to making your book work. If you hadn't hit the problem, you'd never know where to go.

Work-in-progress blocks fall into two subsets:

1. The work itself
2. The author's current skill level to complete that work

All the work we do requires us to rise to the level needed to complete it. Most serious writers don't want to keep doing the same kind of work over and over. They want to push at the boundaries of their art. Language, what can you do? Story, how can you work? We want to grow as writers and artists, and to do that, we have to take narrative risks. We have to try things we've never tried before and be willing to begin all over again. We have to be willing to be humble at the feet of our art. Artists are always learning lest they become stale. They are willing, no matter how many books they've written, to try something new and risk it not working. Expect rough patches. Expect the ideas not to come together as you pictured them. That doesn't mean they aren't coming together in a much better way. Meander. A lot of magic is found along the path.

Remember:

» Keep an open mind toward learning.
» Let the challenge of a craft block force you to experiment with new things.
» Keep going. Make notes so you can see issues arising.
» Avoid going back and reworking in an early draft. Let the early draft do its job: get you to the next draft.

I want you to consider which type of block you're currently experiencing because it will help you better identify and name where you are and inquire as to where you need to go. You're creating a GPS coordinate to work from and creating actionable steps forward. If you feel amorphous, just generically "stuck," you may opt to do nothing. We can't accurately assess a situation we can't identify. Since we are here to move deeper into writer's block to uncover its gifts, we need this clarity to ask some questions. Chapter 5 explores the Deep Inquiry questions you will use.

DEEP INQUIRY PRACTICE

Who Are You?

What type of block brought you to this book? If you're not sure, use these questions to explore which type it may be:

> » What was I writing before I became blocked?
> » What themes were being revealed?
> » What's the next thing that needs to happen in the book (scene, chapter, and so on)?
> » Where do I see the book in the world?
> » What will my parents think of the book?
> » Where do I feel most uneasy with this book?
> » What is different about this book from others I have written?
> » What do I hope this book will bring to me or do for me?
> » What do I hope this book will bring to others?

You can use the insights you gain here to explore one of the dialogue options offered in the next chapter.

5 | Learn to Dialogue with Your Work

Sometimes the simplest and most profound shifts occur when we simply ask questions. Deep Inquiry is the heartbeat of this book. It also provides a path into the heartbeat of your book. Questions stretch your work alive. They create conditions of respect and trust between you and your work. Your willingness to listen gives your work permission to thrive.

To dialogue with your work, you need to employ some skills that come naturally to most writers—personification, character creation, and active imagination. If you accept the premise that everything you encounter in your writing contains a potential gift, then inquiring into the nature of that gift becomes a natural extension of your continued communication with your writing. You can use the very tools and talents that help you write to move through a block.

Let's begin by reframing how you might encounter writer's block and how you might feel in the middle of it. Rather than viewing the block as a problem to be solved, let's look at it as a chance to grow—both as a writer and within your work. The previous chapter discussed differences between work-in-progress blocks and writer-in-process blocks. This distinction was simply to help you narrow your focus for a line of inquiry. If all you feel is "stuck" or "blocked," it can be difficult to unpack the secrets living in this vital time in the writing process. The devil—and the genius—really are in the details and specificity you can bring to all aspects of your work. Identifying the type of block you may be encountering gives you a starting point. Regardless of the type of block you're working with, the Deep Inquiry Dialogue Practice works the same way. We'll begin with general guidelines and then move into specific examples for various elements you may want to address.

DEEP INQUIRY DIALOGUE PRACTICE

Sit comfortably in your writing area. Soften your body, mind, and breath. Take a few full inhalations and exhalations, and breathe into any areas of tension in your body. When you feel ready, begin with personification and characterization of the element you'd like to communicate with. Take out paper and pen or pencil, and draw a quick sketch of this element (fear, dramatic challenge, structure, and so on). Draw this element as a face, a shape, an animal—anything that feels right. You don't need pages and pages of backstory or a degree in art. Work quickly and in the present moment. You're simply creating a visual representation of the entity to whom you'll be talking. Give it a name, if you like.

Next, you're going to use active imagination to embody this character. This is the same approach you use when creating characters in fiction. You'll use empathy and imagination to move into the character you've just created, and from that place, you'll be responding and asking questions.

The questions in the following practices will consistently and compassionately move you through a block. They are here to help you create a dialogue and foster communication with your writing—not to force you to take dictation or give direction. You're using inquiry to help you understand more about the blocks you're experiencing and explore ways your work can help you move forward. You're providing a voice for an aspect of your work and an aspect of yourself, and by learning to listen to the wisdom that is within you, you'll empower your work and integrate your being.

Work-in-Progress Blocks

First, identify the area that needs work (such as Jane's scene with her mother). Personify that issue. Draw a picture if you like. Stick with *one* issue at a time. If you combine them, you'll muddy the results. We want clarity and specificity. For example, "Jane needs to convince her aging mother that she's not able to do everything on her own anymore."

Now you're going to enter into a dialogue with this issue. First, the conversation will be from your perspective. The respondent will be the story itself. If it's possible, I recommend doing these activities with a pen or pencil and paper rather than on a keyboard. Because the act of writing by hand is a form of doodling, physical lettering helps to release tension in your body and mind.

Dialogue Example between Author and Work-in-Progress Element

This first dialogue is between you as the author and one of your work-in-progress elements, such as a scene question, a character challenge, or a structure question. I will write out the questions; after each, pause to allow your work-in-progress to answer. Imagine falling into a conversational flow with your work-in-progress. Use the visual sketch and personification of your element from the previous page to help you embody the character of your block. Ask your work-in-progress:

» What do you need?
» How can I help?
» What is the emotional heart of this work-in-progress element?
» Does anything need to be removed or added in order for this work-in-progress element to be resolved? Feel free to reword as needed to fit the specific element you're working with.
» Is there anything else you can tell me right now?

When you feel complete, be sure to offer gratitude for the exchange, regardless of the outcome.

Do this with any structural or craft-based issue you may have. As you can see, the questions will help you access your work from a different doorway. You can also use these questions, or variations of your own, in a more holistic way. When you've finished a draft or chapter and you want guidance for the next steps, you can ask questions of the larger project.

Don't be afraid of what you might find out. If you learn that you need to develop more craft skills, then take the initiative to do that. That's not a failing. It's a sign of growth. There are many resources at the back of the book for craft assistance. Remember, talent only gets you part of the way. Craft makes talent sparkle.

Please feel free to create your own questions. You are your own best teacher.

Writer-in-Process Blocks

First, draw a quick picture of your writing (whatever you consider to be the entity you're in relationship with when writing). Name it. Personify it in any way you like (color, texture, gender, and so on). You'll be using this personification of your writing to communicate with in the following dialogues. Remember that the way you "see" your writing today may be different from yesterday. Your writing's personification is a fluid creation.

Dialogue Example between Author and Writing

This example has two parts. In the first part, you, the author, are asking the questions and your writing is responding. In the second part, you'll reverse roles and your writing will be asking questions of you. As the author, ask your writing:

» What do you need?
» How can I help?
» How will you feel when you get what you need?

Now switch perspectives and let your writing ask you the same questions.

Sample Conversation with Project, Writing, and Author

Another approach is to work with the specific project, your writing, and you.

If you haven't already drawn a picture of your writing, do that first. Then, draw a quick picture of your specific project. Name it. Personify it in any way you like (color, texture, gender, and so on). The first dialogue will be between you as the author and your project. Ask your project:

» What do you need?
» How can I help?
» How will you feel when you get what you need?

The second dialogue reverses the roles. Your project assumes the role of the interviewer, with you, the author, responding to its questions. Use the same inquiry questions as above.

The third dialogue will be between your writing and the project you are working on. The author is not in this particular exchange. Your writing asks your project:

» What do you need?
» How can I help?
» How will you feel when you get what you need?

The fourth dialogue reverses the roles. This time, the project itself asks the questions and your writing answers. Use the same questions as above.

In the fifth dialogue, you as the author enter the conversation. The first conversation is between you and your writing. You ask your writing:

» What do you need?
» How can I help?
» How will you feel when you get what you need?

In the sixth dialogue, the roles are reversed. Use the same questions, allowing your writing to interview you.

Note how this approach allows insight to come from all aspects of your writing ecosystem—you, the writing itself, and the project you're working on.

Dialogue Example: Author, Writing, and Fear

If you're challenged by a particular fear surrounding your writing, you can apply the same techniques to dive deeper into the gifts of that fear.

Draw a quick picture of your writing. Name it. Personify it in any way you like (characteristics, color, texture, and so on). As the author, you begin the conversation with your writing using our Deep Inquiry Questions:

» What do you need?
» How can I help?
» How will you feel when you get what you need?

Allow your writing to respond.

Now, draw a quick picture of the fear you're working with. Again, give it a name and assign it any characteristics you like. You're going to write a dialogue between the writing and the fear. The writing kicks off as the interviewer, with the fear responding. Use our Deep Inquiry Questions:

» What do you need?
» How can I help?
» How will you feel when you get what you need?

Then, reverse the conversation. Let your fear ask questions of the writing. Use the Deep Inquiry Questions.

And finally, you as the author enter the conversation. This final pairing is between you and the fear you selected. You ask your fear:

» What do you need?
» How can I help?
» How will you feel when you get what you need?

Then, reverse roles, allowing the fear to ask you these questions.

If you're writing these out by hand, it can help to respond using your nondominant hand. When you finish the dialogues, remember to offer gratitude for the work and the experience.

I encourage you to take breaks as you need to between the rounds of questions. Energetic work can be quite emotional. You may also want to engage in some movement practice between the rounds. Even something as simple as shaking out your hands and arms and clapping can help disperse any tension that may have built up as you were engaged in the work. Feel free to draw any responses that arise for you as well. You can also take ownership of your creative process and make your own line of inquiry questions.

Listen to what you hear when you step back and allow the work to speak through you. The responses will reconnect you with what matters.

6 | Release Perfectionism's Chains

Perfectionism is a pattern of behavior that impacts many creative people. It cloaks itself in standards and achievement, masquerading as someone who cares about your work and your career—someone who pushes you to excellence and makes you try just a little bit harder. On its shiny, screaming surface, it looks noble. It seems to have your best interests at heart. But ask any perfectionist how much of an ally it is. Ask how it tries to keep you enslaved to something completely unattainable. How it whispers in your ear, "not good enough, not good enough, not good enough." Perfectionism holds you in its grip and keeps you from moving forward and releasing your work. It is the shadow side of excellence. When your own high standards turn toxic, and your efforts to create the best work possible stop you from creating and sharing anything at all, you can find yourself stuck.

If you find yourself in this type of relationship with perfectionism, you know it right away. You know you're carrying something toxic. Remember, a pattern is only a pattern. It isn't you. Step back from the story line of needing to be perfect, and inquire into the nature of the gift hidden inside the behavior. Perfectionism that goes unexamined and is allowed to run amok becomes a jailor. It will keep you in suspended animation because you know (and you *do* know this intellectually) you can't be perfect. You can't write the perfect book, the perfect poem, or the perfect article. Not because you're not a capable writer, but because perfectionism, in its shadow form, is unattainable. It cannot be achieved. But that doesn't prevent the part of you that believes it can be from knocking at your heart. It then closes you down and prevents you from sharing your work with the world. It prevents you from taking risks. But most of all, it prevents you from growing. Perfectionists rarely finish anything because, well, it's not perfect enough yet, and so it holds you hostage. Perfectionism may also be a manifestation of fear, a feeling of not being good enough or being unworthy, or of not wanting to be seen.

With every behavior you notice in yourself, ask questions: Is this serving me? How? If it isn't, how can I shift it? Take care not to judge yourself for having perfectionist tendencies. Remember that perfectionism is the shadow. Caring about the quality and integrity of your work is the gift. When the desire for excellence goes into overdrive, perfectionism kicks in and you'll shut down. If we believe that all of our behaviors, even the ones that don't work, are in some way attempting to serve us, we can soften to them, delve deeper, and listen to the hidden messages. Let's release perfectionism's chains and transform them into tools that can help you.

DEEP INQUIRY PRACTICE

Getting to Know Your Patterns

Let's start with some Inner Journal questions:

> » How does perfectionism manifest for me?
> » Where do I feel it in my body?
> » When I encounter it, what do I do?
> » What thoughts are associated with this behavior pattern?

When you feel like you have a better sense of the characteristics of your unique perfectionism, take out a piece of paper and make a sketch of it. It can be a human shape, an animal shape, a geometric shape, or a blob of color—anything that feels right to you. Give it a name if you like. Then begin a dialogue with it by asking it these questions:

> » What do you need?
> » How can I help?

Write down its responses in its own voice.

Now, switch places. Have perfectionism ask you the same questions:

» What do you need?
» How can I help?

Uncover what your perfectionism needs, and you'll be on your way to transforming this behavior into a trusted friend.

PART TWO **To Move through a Block**

When you come out of the storm you won't
be the same person who walked in.

That's what the storm is all about.

— *Haruki Murakami*

7 | Welcome Your Writing

Clean, clear, and prepare space for your writing. This may sound silly and rudimentary, but you create welcoming energy for your writing by preparing a space for it to show up. You do not need to build a room onto your house. You don't have to annex the kids' rooms or rent a hotel room. This isn't about the size of your living space or the amount of money you can spend on decorating. It's about the depth of your commitment. Space is measured in energy and intention—not in square feet. You can use a corner of the dining room table. Stephen King, in his book *On Writing,* talks about writing underneath the staircase. You can write in the library. At a coffee shop. On the train. By creating a special place in your life for your work, you will be better able to do the work in that place and bring that work forward into the world.

Wherever you set up your space, make sure it's something you can maintain—in other words, don't choose a space in which you'll constantly be wrestling with a family member. Experiment with different places. Sometimes you might think you've found the perfect space, only to discover that you're not as comfortable there as you'd hoped. That's OK. Flexibility is the watchword of the day. You don't have to keep going back to a place that doesn't work. Try a different location. Shift the direction of your desk if you can. Write in public. Write at home. Write outdoors. Find *your* place, knowing there may be several places. I frequent two public places: the library at a local college where I'm not employed and my favorite coffee shop. I found these places through trial and error. Still, I sometimes shake things up and try a different location just to see what happens. You never know.

Working deeply with yourself and your work is not a forty-eight-hour process. It's something that will only be finished when you release your last breath. It's not linear or outcome based. But it's real, it's substantive, and it will help you build your foundation. Honor your writing. Create the conditions that will allow it to thrive. Welcome it and invite it to stay.

DEEP INQUIRY PRACTICES

The exercises here can be used as quick and easy grounding tools throughout your writing life to help you return to your body and writing. I'll be sharing other physical practices throughout the book, but these two—Balancing Breath and Writer's Mudra—will quickly shift your energies and help you gain a different perspective on your current place in your work's path. They require no special tools or abilities.

Balancing Breath

If you've read either of my earlier writing books—*Writing Begins with the Breath* or *The Writing Warrior*—you already know that I place great value on the breath as an anchor to a writing practice. I want to continue that path in this book by sharing the breathing technique I call Balancing Breath. It's derived from *tu gu na xin*, the ancient Taoist's Six Healing Breaths practice. *Tu gu na xin* is Chinese for "exhaling the old, inhaling the new." This activity helps you do that.

Find a comfortable, quiet place. You can sit or stand. If you're sitting in a chair, make sure your feet rest flat on the floor. If you're seated on the floor, make sure your hips are above your knees, placing a cushion underneath you, if necessary. If you're standing, place your feet slightly more than hip-width apart. Relax your knees and sink your weight into your feet. No matter what position you're in, connect with the energy of the earth through the soles of your feet or the backs of your legs and thighs.

Softly close your eyes. Start by relaxing your upper body and inhaling deeply. At the top of the inhalation, pause for a moment to feel the sense of fullness. Slowly exhale all the air from your lungs. Feel free to make a sound or sigh that feels good as you exhale. On your next inhalation, reach your arms out in front of you, turning your palms toward you. Inhale through your nose. As the breath enters your body, bring your arms back toward your nose and mouth, keeping your palms facing you.

When you're ready to exhale, turn your palms outward, and as you exhale, slowly extend your hands away from you. Exhale through your mouth, with your lips in a soft *O*, as if you're blowing through a straw. Try to keep the breath as silent as you can. Think about it this way: The inhalation is the yin aspect; it's passive. The exhalation is the yang aspect; it's active. When you inhale, you're offering space to receive the breath. The inhalation is simply the natural result of the exhalation.

The key things to remember are to inhale through your nose and exhale through your mouth as silently as possible. Your palms travel toward you on the inhalation and gently press away from you on the exhalation.

Writer's Mudra

A mudra is a hand gesture. The word *mudra* means "to seal." Mudras have a central role in yogic traditions and Indian cultures, but Westerners also use them, even if we don't use the word in general conversation. When people place their palms together in prayer, they're creating a mudra. When they make the thumbs-up sign, they're creating a mudra. In Western yoga classes, you may have used mudras to help channel energy into your body and mind. Mudras have many different meanings and purposes, from tonifying and balancing the body and mind to storytelling in Indian dance practices. The Writer's Mudra described here is a simple moving meditation that you can use at any time to center yourself, regroup, and reconnect with your writing and your work. I'll refer to it frequently in this book, and I encourage you to practice it now as a way of invitation—a way of welcoming your writing into your world, exactly as you both are. Right here. Right now.

Find a comfortable, quiet place. You can sit or stand. If you're sitting in a chair, make sure your feet rest flat on the floor. If you're seated on the floor, make sure your hips are above your knees, placing a cushion underneath you, if necessary. If you're standing, place your feet slightly more than hip-width apart. Relax your knees and sink your weight into your feet. No matter what position you're in, connect with the energy of the earth through the soles of your feet or the backs of your legs and thighs.

Close your eyes and relax your jaw. You may want to stretch your jaw—opening and closing your mouth, shifting your jaw left and right to loosen it. Let your breath naturally slow and soften. Feel the breath's substance as it travels through your nostrils, into your chest and lungs, your belly rising with each inhalation and releasing with each exhalation.

For this first practice, set an intention of simply connecting with your writing. You can create your own intentions as you see fit once you've gotten comfortable with the mudra itself. If you're right-handed, your right hand is going to represent you, the writer, and your left hand is going to represent the writing itself. If you're left-handed, your left hand will represent you and your right hand will represent your writing.

Slowly raise your hands, palms up as if you were making an offering. At your own pace, bring your palms together, creating the physical and symbolic meeting of you and your writing. You may want to pause, palms close but not touching, and feel the energetic heat between your hands. You can separate your palms and bring them back together, playing with the energy field that's dancing between them. When you join your palms, you're creating the prayer gesture, known in Sanskrit as Anjali Mudra, or Pranamasana (Prayer Pose). Remain with this physical meeting of you and your writing as long as you like.

When you're ready to separate your hands, start by rubbing your palms together to create heat. When you feel the energy building up between them, slowly separate your hands and lightly cover your eyes with your palms, breathing in the warmth of the connection you just made. Then place your palms on your voice box, allowing the warm energy to fill your throat. Finally, place your palms over your lower belly, known as your *dantian*. This is the area of the lower abdomen below your navel. The *dantian* is generally considered to be about a third of the way into the abdominal cavity. Think of it as an energy center, similar to a chakra. Use relaxed awareness to bring your attention to this area as you soak in the effects of the connection. When you feel complete, rejoin your palms in front of your heart, lower your head to meet your hands, and offer gratitude.

8 | Learn to See the Gifts of Each Writing Session

Learning to focus on what a writing session offered you rather than what it didn't can help you keep perspective on your work. The twins of attachment and expectation surface frequently in the writing process. You get attached to a result and expect to be able to achieve that precise goal. When you don't, frustration sets in, and depending on your personality, that frustration can quickly spiral into enough self-doubt and negativity to make you get up and walk away, sometimes never to return to the project. It's almost as if, in the Land of Magical Thinking, you feel that if you start a brand-new project, you can avoid the work your writing is calling you to do. Whether you are a writer who is easily frustrated in your sessions or usually find joy in the creative process, setting realistic goals and incorporating a gratitude practice will help you see more of the gems your work is offering you.

Realistic Goal Setting

Goals and objectives are important. It's how we move forward on track and on time. Sometimes, though, our goals are not realistic for where we are in the process—either the book's development (work-in-progress) or our own development as writers (writer-in-process). For example, my first goal with this chapter is to handwrite (my method of choice for early drafting) all my ideas for how to address the topic. I use questions such as, What key points do I want to make? What activities will be most helpful? Nothing gets left out in this draft. If it shows up, I write it down. That's draft one. And no one but me ever needs to see it. Then I walk away from the chapter for a day or two. My next goal will be to see what I gathered during draft one. I ask questions such as, What's useful? What belongs somewhere else? What am I unclear about? What new ideas surfaced? I move forward in this fashion until I get a tight, clean chapter. Then it's time for input from my readers.

This is just one way of modeling realistic goals in a drafting process. Notice that the goal for my first draft was not to have polished work. The objectives I set for each session are in harmony with the stage of development the work is in. If I tried to create a final draft at the same time I tried to figure out what the chapter is actually about, I'd surely get stuck.

We experience frustration through the lens of what did not work relative to our expectations. If we see a session only through what we did not achieve, it will be very difficult to notice the gifts that session did offer. Those gifts, which are often the unexpected piece of magic the work needs, get buried beneath the frustration of thwarted expectations. What if you believed that every writing session provided value? What if you believed that every draft, no matter how rough, provided a gift? How would that simple reframe start to create more softness, openness, and ease toward your writing?

DEEP INQUIRY PRACTICE

Pregratitude Ritual

Find a comfortable, quiet place. You can sit or stand. If you're sitting in a chair, make sure your feet rest flat on the floor. If you're seated on the floor, make sure your hips are above your knees, placing a cushion underneath you, if necessary. If you're standing, place your feet slightly more than hip-width apart. Relax your knees and sink your weight into your feet. No matter what position you're in, connect with the energy of the earth through the soles of your feet or the backs of your legs and thighs.

Close your eyes and relax your jaw. You may want to stretch your jaw—opening and closing your mouth, shifting your jaw left and right to loosen it. Let your breath naturally slow and soften. Feel the breath's substance as it travels through your nostrils, into your chest and lungs, your belly rising with each inhalation and releasing with each exhalation. Complete three rounds of Balancing Breath, then move into your version of Writer's Mudra. As you join your palms, creating the connection between you and your writing, offer a word of thanks—a word of "pregratitude" for the gifts of the time you'll spend together.

We are conditioned to offer thanks after we've received something. By offering gratitude before anything has happened, we help create an open channel between ourselves and our writing. We shift our expectations of the writing session from something rigid to something wondrous. We are more open to the possibilities of what could happen instead of comparing what does happen to what we've planned.

To close the practice, bring your palms together at your heart. Inhale deeply and on the exhalation, bow your head to your heart.

Gathering Gifts

After you've taken a break from drafting and are ready to return to the work, try this. Read through what you wrote without editing. Make notes of surprises, funny lines, things that worked, things you weren't expecting. Reading through this way first will start to train you to see hidden treasures before you focus on flaws or places that need improvement. You may want to keep a separate list in your journal of these surprise gifts so you can start to see them accumulating.

This activity is rooted in how you see your work. Can you look underneath the expectations you may have had and see the glimmers of potential? This can be very challenging and beneficial for writers who are particularly critical of themselves and their work. Remember that writing unfolds in stages. This practice can also help uncover unexpected directions and depths in your work. You'll be able to see a cumulative effect of surprises and gifts in the lists you're making. Remember, the gifts are always present. We must cultivate the eyes to see them.

Compassion Practice

When it feels like nothing's really working on a particular day, reach outside yourself into the larger literary conversation. What's one thing you can do for the health of books, of stories, of writers? This could be buying a book from an independent bookseller, attending a reading, or reading to your child. What feels like sacred service that benefits the literary world? This practice can help you see the gifts that writing brings to the larger world and remember why what you are doing matters.

9 | Maintain Motivation

There is a distinct link between practice and achievement. But to maintain a practice, we need motivation. Let's look at three qualities necessary to motivate people to show up for their creative practice: autonomy, value, and competence.

The perception of having autonomy, of being in control of your choices, is linked to the amount of energy you apply to your goals. If you feel forced to do something, you will not be as inclined to give your best efforts. When people feel they have autonomy, their motivation increases. Keeping track of your practice and using the 49-day powersheets in the appendix will help you gain this feeling of autonomy over your own time and creative choices. Holding and maintaining flexible boundaries helps as well.

Embracing the value of what we do can be tricky for writers. Our work isn't always tangible to others, and if our circle of friends can't see the reason for our efforts, it's sometimes hard for us to see it ourselves. Value in our work is connected to our hopes for our writing. Often, writers get stuck on a hoped-for outcome for their work: the *New York Times* bestseller list, a huge social media following, a lucrative movie deal. Focusing on those outcomes can diminish the pleasure the creative act itself gives the writer. The current activity is measured against a not-yet-realized external goal. When you recognize that as a writer you need to write to be in balance, you start to see the value in the act of simply writing. The outcome becomes secondary. Shifting value from an external result you can't control to an internal process practice over which you have some influence can make all the difference. You feel the act of writing filling your soul, just like you feel its absence when you neglect it.

When people believe what they're doing has value—for themselves or others—their level of engagement in the activity increases. Even if you're doing something you "have to do," such as an assignment for work or school, if you can find a way to make it meaningful to you—to find value in it—you'll apply yourself more fully. You'll experience less tension and resistance to the work as well.

Finally, there is competence. Of course, being proficient at something tends to increase our enjoyment of an activity. We naturally want to spend time with things for which we show some aptitude. However, competence increases with practice. The more attention we give something, the greater our skills become. Interestingly, people who believe that innate talent is more important than consistent practice tend to give up more quickly. They can easily believe they aren't talented enough, which is far more palatable than admitting they aren't committed enough. I can practice singing all day every day, and I'll still never have Adele's voice. But I will improve—and if singing gives me pleasure, it doesn't matter that I'll never get a record contract. The value, to me, is in the act of singing.

Autonomy, value, and competence are qualities we can cultivate. There are no fixed or predetermined amounts of each element for each writer. As we learn to own and commit to our choices, as we come to understand the value writing provides us simply by its presence in our lives, and as we study the craft and tools available to help us bring our writing alive, we can move into greater ease in our writing lives.

DEEP INQUIRY PRACTICE

Exploring the Elements

The three traits of autonomy, value, and competence can surface when we are faced with writer's block. Here are some initial inquiry questions you can pose when you find yourself stuck:

» Do I see any value in doing this? If not, what would give this value?

» Do I feel forced to do this? If so, how can I reclaim a sense of autonomy (for example, adjust my writing schedule or reframe the project's requirements)?

» Do I feel this project exceeds my competence? If so, what steps can I take to learn more about the art and craft of writing?

10 | Cultivate Healthy Boundaries

If I had to list the top reasons people give for why they don't finish, start, or revise their work, some variation on how they relate to time always makes the cut. Time is not a tangible thing. Perhaps the challenges lie in the unknown of it all, which may make time more difficult to relate to than a fixed amount of money in the bank or a certain number of frequent flier miles. We can only count our days in reference to those we've already lived, and then we make our best guesses at what's to come. Who knows how many hours and days we have left? It's difficult to contemplate the end of our lives, so sometimes we move through them, not taking agency of the days we have. Time, that pesky thing—let's just brush it under the rug. We'll think about it later.

Let's look at some common misconceptions about time:

1. There is no universe in which you always get to do what you want when you want. Holding out for this mythical place is wasted energy. Life has obligations—work, family, self-care. These obligations are not invisible or unimportant. They won't disappear. That magical place where all your needs are met by unicorns does not exist. Don't pretend like it does. This myth manifests in statements such as the following:

» When I win the lottery . . .
» When the kids are grown . . .
» When I retire . . .
» When my parents are well . . .
» When _____ happens . . .

This myth creates a false separation between you and your writing. It tells your writing to stay back—at arm's length—that it has nothing to offer you *now*. I pose these questions: Why choose to live a life without using one of your abilities? Why shut a part of yourself away? Writing isn't a one-way street. It can help you be a more fully alive and awake person today. It doesn't need to wait for some distant time in the future when you think all the planets have aligned. Use the lineup you have today.

2. You aren't responsible for every aspect of the lives of other people. Yes, if you're a parent, you have certain responsibilities to your child, but you do not have to hover. You aren't responsible for your spouse or partner's happiness. You can't control those things. You can't live another person's life. Sometimes people absorb the lives of others because it seems easier than carving out a life of their own. Claim your own life. Put the oxygen mask on yourself before assisting others. You have nothing to offer if you are depleted.

3. Writing isn't a selfish waste of time. I've heard this one so many times it hurts. There is nothing "more productive" you need to be doing. Making things—creating things—is a high calling.

The perfect time is today. Nothing will be more perfect tomorrow or when circumstances are different. You don't have to wait for the first of the month or the first of the week. Today is the day. Why? Because today is the day you embody.

Setting Healthy Boundaries

Think of a boundary as a flexible barrier. You control the level of flexibility but not who or what is on the other side. Something unexpected will *always* come up. Someone will always ask you to do one more thing, serve on one more committee, pick up one more job. That's the nature of life. Expecting a time when that won't occur is a fantasy. Waiting for others to stop asking things of you is like trying to stop a freight train with a feather.

To set healthy boundaries, begin by taking inventory of what you do in a given day. What must you do (to keep a roof over your head, stay healthy, and so on)? What do you choose to do? For each choice, ask yourself how that activity is serving you. Select and deselect activities according to how they meet your goals. No one is telling you to quit your job. We all have things we must do. Leave those "musts" alone, and focus on the chosen activities. (You know you don't really have to attend that party of a friend-of-a-friend-of-a-friend!)

Setting strong boundaries is a form of self-care. You aren't creating a fence to keep the world out. You're taking care of yourself so you can move more fully and consciously in the world. Setting healthy boundaries also requires you to let go of needing to please anyone. It's not about being mean or snarky. It's about respecting yourself. Just because someone asks you to do something, you don't have to do it. Live and make choices in integrity with what serves your highest self. It doesn't matter if the whole world likes you (it won't). It matters that you like yourself, and from this place of self-love, you more fully embrace the world. Understand what you need in your life to feel whole. Find the value in your work. Get your house in order. You cannot do it all or have it all. You have to choose. Choose wisely.

If you want to make changes in your boundaries, ask for support. Let your friends and family know what you're doing. Most of us have commitments to other human beings as well as our writing. We're not solely able to rest on our desert island with our work. We have families, obligations at work, friendships to maintain. These things matter and need our attention and care. But if we don't let others know what we're doing, not only may we not have their support, but we may also be swept away by their needs. If you don't tell others what you need, they cannot know. No one can read your mind.

Of course, you can't tell your six-month-old baby not to need you at a certain time. But in our relationships with adults and older children, we can set clear boundaries and ask that they be respected. The more specific you are with your intentions, the easier they will be to implement. Let your family know you will be unavailable for thirty minutes or an hour and are not to be disturbed. Be clear on where and when you'll be doing your writing, and share with them how important it is to you. If you have children, you are modeling healthy boundaries and good self-care for them. This not about neglecting your responsibilities. It is about filling your soul with what's important to you so you have a full heart to share with those you love.

Learning to Say No

Practice saying no to things that don't bring you into greater harmony with your writing. Again, I'm not saying tell your boss to take this job and shove it if you have obligations to meet. But many people simply say yes to anything and everything—not out of a genuine desire to do those things, but out of a resistance to conflict. When you're asked to do something, check in with yourself first: Is this something I actually want to do? Would engaging in this activity bring value to my life (friendship, family time, outdoor activities, and so forth), or would it drain my energy? What does my heart want?

Here are a few things to remember about saying no:

» No is a complete sentence. You do not have to explain your reasoning.
» A yes means nothing if you can't hold your no. You can't say yes fully if you can't also say no.
» No is not a rejection of a person or an activity. Saying no in one area of your life allows you to say yes to something else.
» Your time is finite. Just like you get to choose what you'll spend your money on, you also get to choose what you spend your time on. Don't spend your time in activities that won't expand your energy.
» It can take practice to say no, especially if you're a person who likes to please others. Practice. It's worth it.
» No is a means of effective boundary setting. Remember, no one else can or will hold your boundaries for you. They are your responsibility to maintain.
» Don't make the mistake of believing there will be more time later. The time you have is right now. Build the fences you need around the time required to do the work you're meant to do.

Procrastination

Procrastination is a form of self-sabotage, and it contributes to our frustrations with our dreams for our writing. When everything is put off until the last minute, nothing gets done well and the tension of what we're not doing overshadows anything we think we might be gaining from procrastination. Procrastination is often a by-product of feeling overwhelmed, which can come from not having a clear sense of what we need and choose to do. It's easier (or seems easier) not to do anything until the deadline, and the rush of adrenaline we get under stress contributes to the "I perform better under pressure" myth. Evidence does not support this thinking. We can get addicted to the endorphin rush that occurs with the last-minute release, which further binds us to self-destructive behavior patterns.

Don't live your life in a state of heightened tension. The softer you are, the more fluidly you can move.

DEEP INQUIRY PRACTICE

Time Use Log

Keep track of what you do for seven days. Unlike the Powersheets in the appendix, this exercise asks you to record everything you do in a given day, not just the time you spend writing. Use a chart to block out all twenty-four hours of every day. A format similar to a Day-by-Day calendar that will allow you to block off time in fifteen-minute increments might be useful. What do you do during each of those hours? No judgment here. You're gathering baseline data. After your week is up, evaluate the results. Where do you spend the most time? Is it where you want to be? If not, what can you adjust? You may want to make a bar or pie chart of time use to help you see visually where most of your day goes. These results aren't set in stone. Adjust what you need to. To change something, we have to first understand what we're doing. If you learned you watch twelve hours of Netflix on Saturdays, and that's not something you want to be doing, you've gained a great insight. Don't tear yourself down. Use the information you've gathered to build yourself up.

11 | Be at Ease with the Creative Process

The creative process is not a fixed set of steps. It's not a recipe or a formula. It won't yield the same results for every person. It won't even yield the same results for the same person day to day. The creative process isn't a machine. It's the ocean in which artists must swim to bring forth their work. It is unique, impossible to reproduce, and more than a touch magical. We can understand it as a living body of water, a constantly moving, flowing creation that nurtures our project along. Our job as creative artists—as writers—is to establish the conditions conducive to caring for this project and this ocean. We show up with regularity, observe what is occurring without judgment, and do the next right thing.

You may have been taught that the writing process is a series of actions: draft, revise, edit, submit—or something to that effect. This formula is the basis for freshman composition classes all across the country. And it's useful. Yes, you have to draft. Yes, you have to revise. Yes, you have to edit (which is not the same as revision), and yes, if you want anyone to read it, you have to submit it somewhere. But these steps are physical actions that a writer takes. They are outflow, outward reaching, yang. There's a yin part to the writer's process as well. There's a hidden part that must occur so that the outward manifestations of the process can be effective. Writer's block lives in the yin space, underneath the visible harvest, in the foundation space that holds the whole thing together.

Let's reframe the writing process as something more holistic and animated. It is not a series of fixed, dead steps like boxes to check off or lines to color within. It may be more beneficial to think of the writing process as a symphony with a variety of movements, pauses, crescendos, and decrescendos, with a unifying theme even if the listener doesn't realize it until the final note. In music, we can recognize that there is movement even in the silence, the pause. We can feel that pause as something necessary that holds all the notes together. In that symphony spirit, let's delineate the creative process in terms of movements. I'm intentionally not numbering them so you will be less likely to think of them chronologically. All these movements can occur multiple times during any creative project and in a variety of sequences. Although it's unfair to think of the writing process as an unyielding entity, and I don't want to promote the idea of a formula, it is helpful to have some common language to discuss the themes in the process.

Movements of the Creative Process

Stillness: Stillness can feel like nothing is happening at all. You've hit that wall. You have nothing left. Remember that everything must rest. It's in the resting that we rejuvenate and prepare ourselves for the next thing. This is a time to empty out and be with that space long enough to choose what you want to bring in. It's a time to reflect on what you've made and tune into what might be on its way to you. This place often feels itchy. Try not to scratch too soon.

Gathering: When we gather, we accumulate anything and everything that catches our intuitive writer's eye and ear. We take notes. We draft some pages that don't seem to have any purpose at all. We read books or create playlists. We dream, getting glimmers of a place, hearing fragments of a voice. When you're in this movement, remain a nonjudgmental observer. Don't try to predetermine what you need and don't need.

Pausing: A pause differs from stillness. How? Stillness is the time before the symphony begins and after it's over—before we know we have a writing project or just after we've finished one. The last note reverberates. We can't see the next thing. A pause, however, is the beat between the inhalation and the exhalation. We're midstride in a project. We've got some work behind us, and we know to some extent what's in front of us. We're just taking that breath before we make the next move.

Planting: Here, we draft. And draft, and draft. In our very first draft, we're not trying to make it anything at all. We're just putting things down. We don't know yet what will take root. We don't know yet what word will lead to what word. Our responsibility in this movement is to set forth what we've been given.

Harvesting: We have a finished draft! We can see the proverbial fruits of our labor. What is it? It may not be clear yet, but we have something organic. Something alive. We get to look at it now and see what we grew.

Sorting: What fits? What belongs somewhere else? What do we need to cut? We can't carry everything forward into the finished book. We have to be selective, paring off what isn't the book, remaining grateful that those parts we're culling were there to hold the newly fragile heart of our work safe until we could find it.

Releasing: We have to let some ideas go. Sometimes they go to an agent or editor. Sometimes they go to our writers group. Sometimes they go in the drawer or the file we have of Gifts That Didn't Quite Reach Fruition. No matter where we let our work go, we release it with love and gratitude, with hopes for it to find its place in the larger literary conversation.

Any one of these movements can send us back to another one. We can sort and then return to plant anew. We can harvest and then be still. One process, many stages. It's a nonlinear path. Think of it like colors in a stained-glass window. Each color on its own doesn't reveal the whole, but when you step back and see the pattern, you gasp at its beauty.

The more experienced you become with your unique method of creation, the more at ease you will feel shifting from movement to movement along the continuum. Embrace the impermanence of each movement, and you'll integrate much more freely with the larger process. You'll see that you are part of a whole, and each segment is essential to the larger organism.

Writer's Stages of Development

Just as our writing moves through stages, we as writers also go through different emotional and mental phases as we work. Writers develop like any other complex organism: over a long period of time, by making many mistakes and false starts, with great love and nurturance, and by employing curiosity. We evolve through each writing session. We are the stone rolling downhill, gathering skills and experiences we can use in our work. We are the newborn, the sage, and the impetuous youth all at once. We can't settle for certainty, but we can't hover on the edge of indecision for too long either.

Every creative project we undertake will teach us unexpected things. We will begin with new, wet eyes, awakening in wonder. We'll grow to jaded adolescence, then cocky twenty-one-year-olds, and we'll mellow out in middle age and our final years. We'll do this over and over. We won't reach a pinnacle and hang out there. Because we're artists, we'll keep pushing ourselves to try new things, and because we try new things, we'll begin again. Fresh eyes. Fresh pen. Fresh stance.

If we can embrace this natural continuum, the suffering that arises when we can't "figure it out" or directly apply what we did figure out in the last project will lessen substantially. Humility is the natural outreach from this understanding, and humility allows for growth and surprises. Just like within every adult lives a toddler-self, within every writer—no matter how long he or she has been writing—lives a beginner, an adolescent, and a sage.

This continuum applies both to the project you're working on *and* to your own development as a writer. Understanding where you fall on the continuum at any point in the writing process can help you maintain commitment. My path frequently follows these lines:

» Innocence
» Arrogance/certainty
» Loss of innocence
» Chaos
» Humility/apprenticeship

What about yours?

The longer I work with writing and the longer I pay attention to myself in relation to that writing, the less likely I am to take any of these stages as permanent and fixed. If you can identify where you fall along your continuum when you get blocked, you can create more meaningful questions and dialogues with your work.

No matter how long I've been writing, I still have to reach the point in my process where I have to surrender the idea of the book and start to cultivate what the actual book is. I'm not as surprised by that these days, but I still hear that tiny voice: "Couldn't you have seen this coming?" Sometimes it's that certainty and arrogance that gets us to the page where we wrestle with what comes next. If we always stayed in doubt, it might be hard to show up for the work. When you can identify the stage you're in, you feel more comfortable about what's next. For example, if you're in the space of certainty (or adolescence), your inquiry into your work might try to direct yourself toward a bit of open space: "Why am I so sure about ____?" or, "What if my protagonist didn't slay that dragon in the fourth chapter? What could happen then?"

Don't strive to perfect anything. Practice presence with what is instead. Your work can't thrive if you hold it up to an impossible standard. It can't thrive if you've predetermined what it must be before it has a chance to be what it actually is.

DEEP INQUIRY PRACTICE

Identify Your Stages of Writing

It may be fun for you to name the continuum stages as you see them. Use the ones I listed in the chapter as a starting point if you need to. Put in as many stages as you like.

Stage 1:
Stage 2:
Stage 3:
Stage 4:
Stage 5:

What adjectives describe how each stage feels? Can you draw an image for each stage? Naming and describing where you are in any given place helps you clarify your surroundings, allowing you to move from the abstract "stuck" into a dimensional place that you can see from your own list is impermanent.

12 | Be Your Own Teacher

Writers have a peculiar challenge. Though we can read books on craft, take classes and workshops, and even work with mentors, no one can actually teach us our own writing process. We have to be able to maintain the bizarre psychic split of being both teacher and student to ourselves. We have to learn to let in the knowledge and advice of those who've gone before us without blindly following their path. Their path is theirs. It cannot also be ours. We must learn to select and reject advice as needed to keep us on our own path of integrity. When we're writing, we're holding the hands of both our teacher-selves and our student-selves. We are teaching ourselves what works for us by trying things on for size. We can adapt what we like as we grow.

As a writing teacher, I can only help my students normalize their own experiences. I offer suggestions and advice, but I can't walk their path for them. If I were crafting a piece of furniture, my students could watch me select the wood, use the tools, and transform the wood into the finished product. They could begin by copying what I did as the first step in their learning. But the real work of writing goes on inside each writer's mind. No one can watch another writer *writing*. We can only watch the typing, and that reveals nothing about the art itself. It is in our best interest—as well as our writing's best interest—to learn how to be both student and teacher. To be comfortable in the mystery that is our own way.

As someone who's been teaching writing for more years than most of my students have been alive, I can assure you that I cringe at the statement, "Writing can't be taught." It can. I do it every day. What can't be taught is how to be a writer, because there is no "a" writer. No single way of working with the tools of writing (the part we can teach you) and no single way of working with the challenges of spending so much time alone in your room.

People ask us at conferences and readings: "When do you write? Do you write longhand or on the computer? Where do you get your ideas?" As if those questions would reveal anything at all about what would work for the person asking. We've been taught to find out how other people do something in order to learn how to do it ourselves. If you were learning to grow roses, you'd read or ask about the best places in the yard to plant them, how often to water them, when they should be pruned, and you'd get a reasonably standard answer. But having a certain pen or a particular brand of laptop isn't what makes a person write well or even write at all. Getting up at dawn or staying up until midnight doesn't make a person a writer. We can watch a chef prepare a meal or a dancer pirouette across the stage. We can listen to the master guitarist play his instrument. We can watch a writer write too, but that's not going to reveal anything other than how many times the writer fidgets, wanders around the room, or cracks his knuckles. The heart of the "where do you get your ideas" questions is, "Can I do this too?" And the honest answer is, "I don't know. Can you?"

We write internally, and the result of all that internal work is an external sentence. Then we work to make that external sentence mesh with what was percolating in our inner world. Therein lies a mighty long road, as my grandfather used to say. The distance between the inner writing and the external manifestation of it is both temporally and emotionally great. The work that makes the writer *write* takes place in silence inside the writer's mind and heart. We don't so much figure out how to do it as we figure out who we are *in relationship* to our work. In other words, we have to learn how we write, who we are as writers, and how writing manifests itself for us. We have to teach ourselves. We are both teacher and student, creator and imitator. We can't copy another writer's process, even if we can articulate it. We can't be anyone but who we are, and that simple fact is the undoing of many wannabe writers. Writing demands that you look inward. If you can do that even when every part of you is screaming to look away, you've got a shot at this gig. I say that as if it were easy. As if anyone could do it. Perhaps anyone can, but everyone doesn't. It's far easier to look away than to stay put. Far easier to deflect, blame, and redirect our attention than to deeply examine our own shadows and light.

A professor or workshop leader can provide many helpful insights and offer up the wisdom of those who've gone before, those who've gotten lost and found, those who've given up. The instructor can provide fresh eyes on your work, explain craft concepts you may not know, and point you in the direction of a whole shelf of authors who might shine a light on your stories through their own casts of characters. But none of us can slip inside your mind and navigate your own inner jungle for you. We can speak to our own jungles, and you may be able to find some camaraderie there, but that's all we can offer. You have to be able to step back from yourself, observe what you're doing—on both the inner landscape and the outer one on the page—without judgment and make adjustments along the way. You've got to self-direct as much as you listen to the advice and opinions of others. And it's here, in that Gordian knot of our inner world, that we get trapped.

We are all writers-in-process all the time, and if we make the mistake of thinking that someone else has the secret potion or the magic wand to do this deep work for us, we'll walk away from our stories and not look back. One of the most difficult things we can do is be still, look deeply within, and stay long enough to see underneath the stories we tell ourselves to keep us from seeing the stories that are truly there.

When I begin any workshop, the first thing I do is listen to what the participants are telling me. I never ask them to tell me their job titles or publication status. I don't want them to identify with those things first, and I don't want others in the workshop to make upward or downward comparisons based on what they perceive other people are or are not doing. I ask them their names and for a word or two that describes their current relationship to their writing. That keeps it real. Keeps it from getting snagged in the shoulda, coulda, woulda places. I'm listening to find out not so much what they say, but what they leave unsaid. The unsaid parts usually filter out as we go around the circle. I watch the body language. I watch the shifting postures. I want to intuit where they are in their process. Something called them to the workshop. I don't have to know what it is, but I need to know how it's kicking around inside them. I want to find the door into each student's process and then hold it open for her to walk through on her own.

DEEP INQUIRY PRACTICES

Generate Your Own Magic

It's easy to get swept up in a new program or a new promise that assures you that if you only do "this one thing" or "these ten steps," then you'll have a completely new life. We see blog posts, magazine articles, and self-help books promising everything from weight loss to financial freedom to true love. Seductive titles sell books. But what happens after the sale? What happens after the reader has tried the steps and nothing is different?

You don't have to look for a teacher or find a program to have tools for your work. You have the power within you to create your own prompts, your own series of meditations that can directly inform and enhance your current work-in-progress. Now that you have an idea about how to use meditation and direct inquiry into your work, what questions come up for you? What prompt ideas can you generate? Store them in your Writer's Drawer. They'll be there when you need them.

Writer Ancestor Guides

Sometimes it can be helpful to have a friend. Someone you can talk to about anything that's going on in your creative life. Someone you can ask anything of. If you could take any writer, living or dead, with you on your journey, who would it be? Why?

Believe it or not, you *can* take this writer with you. You can consult with, cry with, and celebrate with the writer guide of your choice. When you've determined who that would be, find a picture or post-card of them (Google Images is awesome), print it out, and put it in your workspace. Use this writer as both counsel and inspiration. Dialogue with him or her as necessary. Use your nondominant hand as your writer guide to answer your questions. What would Gertrude Stein say? William Faulkner? Anaïs Nin?

You can use your natural imaginative abilities to create a persona for your writer guide and strengthen those conjuring skills you need so much to do your work, while at the same time gaining valuable insight. Of course you're not literally talking to this writer, but you're channeling that person's wisdom and funneling it through yourself. If that's not writing, then I don't know what is.

Guests of Honor

Who or what do you meet on the blank page? When you begin a writing session, who is there with you? Take some time here. You may meet ancestors. Other writers and mentors. Characters. Sides of you that you only reveal during this sacred time. Create a cast list of who is with you at one session. You might like to choose one of your companions and dedicate a writing session to that person. You might also enjoy dialoguing with some of them. If they're with you already, they likely have something to say!

13 | Challenge Your Beliefs about Writing

The things we believe about writing, ourselves as writers, and where our work should be connect to where we may find ourselves stuck. It's a healthy practice to continue to reevaluate what you believe, why you believe it, and whether or not that belief is still serving you. Unchallenged and unchecked beliefs lead to rigidities about what's possible that will block your progress.

Consider the adage of the fish in the bowl. It has no idea it is swimming in water. It doesn't even know there's any such thing as water. Likewise, we don't know all of our hidden motivations. If we can uncover some of those motivations, we can begin to see our work and our relationship to it more clearly.

When Hope Meets Fear

We have so many dreams for our work. As stories germinate inside us, they can take on such rich lives. We can imagine the sentences, the cover design, the blurbs on the dust jacket. We may imagine our stories are going to be the ones that move legions of readers. The ones passed on from generation to generation with the whisper, "Read this one. It mattered to me." Or maybe your dream is to hold a copy in your hand, still warm from your printer, white pages stacked end to end as the ink dries. "I have finished this book," you can say. And no one will ever be able to take that away from you.

What are your hopes for your work? Let's explore this on the micro and macro planes. The micro plane involves your current work-in-progress. The macro plane is your writing life and career. What do you hope for? At the end of your life, what do you want to have done with your writing? And what do you want your writing *itself* to have done? Remember, practice compassion and nonjudgment.

Don't minimize your answers or discount them offhand as impossible. This is no time for practicality. Within our hopes lives our potential. I would love to be a blues singer, but I don't have the pipes for it. But knowing that hope, even if I'm not going to wind up selling out concert halls, reveals something to me. If I can release attachment to it, I can explore what's underneath the hope. For me, that answer lies in a connection to music itself. I want my life to be filled with live music. The human voice moves my heart.

What are you looking for? What do you need? What is the thing you're grasping for actually pointing toward? Is it really the *New York Times* bestseller list? (And that's fine!) Or is it an elusive marker that will mean something for you as a writer? Sometimes the object of our desire is not what we want at all. It is simply the thing onto which we've projected a more secret or hidden want. Something we may not yet have told even ourselves.

The Shadows

Packaged nicely with our hopes are a whole host of shadows—the hidden meanings we make out of our hopes. These shadows get lumped under an umbrella word: *fear,* or perhaps *resistance.* Shadows are pertinent to many aspects of your life. After all, your writing isn't something done by someone else masquerading as you. When a particular hope for your work meets its shadow partner—the fear associated with what that hope will mean—it can cause your writing gears to grind to a halt. These shadow partners may not even be of your own making. They may be beliefs you've gathered along the course of your life from other people's shadows. But no matter where it comes from, the shadow contains the teacher.

In *The Poetry Home Repair Manual,* the former United States Poet Laureate Ted Kooser teaches a concept he calls "noun shadows." He counsels aspiring poets, when selecting a word or image to use in their work, to remember that there are always associations—shadows—that a reader brings to a particular word. He's arguing for specificity, while also cautioning poets that they can never control a reader's response. What may be a beautiful thing to us—say, a butterfly—may have sinister or sad connotations to another person. These shadows affect the way we respond to a text as well. They carry many of the beliefs and impressions we've gathered along the way. One person's idea of fun rarely corresponds to another's. And, as you might guess, these shadows affect our beliefs about writer's block, both in general and when connected to a specific project.

The Tao tells us, "When the guest comes, make hot tea. When the guest leaves, throw it out." This verse is the epitome of clean living. When an emotion arises, let it in. Feel it. Experience it all. And when it leaves, let it go. Clear the house. Clean the space. Beautiful words but very difficult to practice. Many of us have lots of emotions we've gathered and held along the way. In our personal process of our current work, we want to look at what sticky things we've adhered to our writing and our projects. What are the noun shadows of our project? Then, we can determine whether or not we want those things to be there.

Don't get bogged down trying to figure out where these shadows come from—who put them there (you or others), or why they're there. These are head-based reflections that yield little benefit. What matters is what *is* there. What is the direct experience you're having, and do you want to shift it? You can change a pattern without having to analyze where it came from. Don't let your thoughts and your desire to figure out a cause and intellectualize a "felt experience" get in the way of what you need to do. Trying to think too much is often a clue that you aren't yet ready to let the pattern go.

I was once working on a particular pattern with a teacher of mine, and I was really trying to figure out where it came from. It baffled me. He asked, "Does it matter? All that matters now is that you know it's there, and you can make a different choice about how to relate to it."

DEEP INQUIRY PRACTICES

Getting in Touch with the Shadow

Do some Inner Journal writing on these prompts to help you find where your dilemmas may be living. This is just exploratory writing. Only write what arrives—make no judgments.

> » Writing means . . .
> » What do I want to be/do with my writing?
> » When I achieve _____ [answer from preceding question], I will . . .
> » Completing this project means . . .
> » If I don't complete this project, . . .
> » If I don't achieve what I want, it will mean . . .
> » Being a writer means I . . .
> » When I finish this book my (mother/father/significant other) will . . .

Read what you wrote. Do you see any patterns that may be getting in your own way? It's OK if you don't. You just want to pay attention with compassion. Things will reveal themselves as they are able. Here are additional questions to examine:

> » What story am I accepting about myself as a writer?
> » What story am I accepting about this book I am writing?
> » Is it a valid story?
> » If not, what are the steps I can take to rewrite or revise that story?
> » What am I no longer willing to carry with me into the future?

If you're ready to release something, first offer gratitude for all that the story has taught you and bid it a fond farewell. Remember, compassion. Being human is not about perfection. And yes, that also applies to you!

Mining Your Fears for Gold

Make a list of any fears you have about writing, both generally and specifically about your work-in-progress. For now, just be aware. You're writing these lists not to overwhelm yourself and create a sense of dread, but rather to help you gain perspective on what you're working with. The more clearly you can state what you're feeling and experiencing, regardless of whether it's a "negative" or a "positive" feeling, the stronger position you'll be in to make choices for your next steps. When we refuse or can't seem to find the words to articulate what we're feeling, we become overwhelmed. That's when we are no longer sure what's going on. We can't address what we can't define. Imagine trying to find your friend's house in a new neighborhood without an address. You'd just be "feeling" your way through the avenues, hoping somehow you'd guess where her house was among the hundreds that look peculiarly alike. An address, or at the very least an intersection, would be quite helpful. Identifying your fears serves as an address—a place to focus your attention now that you can find it and it's no longer lurking in the shadows of your mind. These lists will evolve as you do. They are a part of you, but they do not define you or your potential.

Remember to practice nonjudgment and compassion. Remember that *everyone* has fears and resistance to things. It's part of being human. Understand that fears, like all things, are transient, and simply having a list so that those fears are no longer swimming amorphously in your mind can help alleviate anxiety.

Now, take another look at the list of fears you created. Choose one fear from your list that speaks to you today. Ask it two questions:

1. What do you need?
2. How can I help?

You can type these answers, but it may be even more helpful to write them out using your nondominant hand as the "fear" responding to you.

14 | Let Go of Being Productive

There's a difference between finishing a book and building pages. We can assemble thousands of pages writing three journal pages each morning, but we won't have a book. We'll have thousands of pages. Many writers confuse production with creation. It's easy to do. If we're not producing something, we're told, we're certainly not creating anything. To learn our craft, we need to practice. We need to generate pages. We need to do this for a very long time. That's an unpopular notion these days, but it remains true. Artists need time to learn the tools of their craft and understand their unique relationship with their art. They need time to learn the tools intimately enough to make them their own. This involves building pages. Some of those pages will by luck turn into a story or two. A poem perhaps. But most of them are doing exactly what they're supposed to be doing: helping us learn our craft and letting us practice. Those two elements come before the book. Trying to do all three at once—learning your craft, cultivating a consistent practice, and writing the Great American Novel—is a recipe for madness. Begin at the beginning, and you'll get where you're going.

Most of us just aren't accustomed to things taking a long time. Our meals don't take a long time anymore. Neither does travel or mail. We can see the faces of friends and family in real time with the touch of a button, no matter where they are on the planet. We keep pushing the envelope on how fast something can be, as if fast were always better than slow. As if there were no value in waiting for anything. No value in creating space between the first glimmer of desire and the fulfillment of that desire.

When writers hit a block, it flies in the face of production. It pulls us up in a dead stop and reminds us that we are not always able to get what we want when we want it. It reminds us to be humble in the throes of creation. It reminds us of the necessity of the pause. It's easy to start to judge the block through the lens of "faster-faster-faster." It's easy to think we're somehow broken because we've reached an abyss.

This pause is only a problem if you're entirely outcome-focused in your sessions, if you're racing to reach an end. The most direct route is not always the right route. It's not always the one that will give you what you need. What if you don't need to be a *producer* of words? What if you returned to a place of play with them instead? What if you returned to deeper observation and deeper communion with the art form? What if, from that place, you created words?

If you make your living with words, it can be easy to forget that you once sought them out because of the pleasure they gave you. You were once amazed, and from that place of amazement, you wanted to immerse yourself in all that words and stories could be. The day-to-day practice of working with language can become tedious if we don't take steps to remain in communion and mutual respect with our work. When we become grown up and responsible, we can forget the importance of play. Of fun. Of finding delight in what we do—and when we do find delight, noticing how our relationship to the time we shape for those activities changes.

If you're a novice writer and struggling with the enormity of the craft or running up against a collision between your expectations and your current abilities, it can be easy to forget that you came to this pursuit because it was fun. It lightened your heart. It was a worthy companion for your time. Return to that place of delight to shift your relationship to your work.

DEEP INQUIRY PRACTICES

Bubble Breathing

A fun way to connect to your breath and lighten your writer's heart is to use Bubble Breathing. Go to the dollar store and buy a kid's bottle of bubbles. Pull out the wand. Remember that smell from childhood?

It's OK, no one is watching. Inhale, and with a full exhalation, blow the bubbles through the wand. Repeat as needed until the lightness has taken over.

Rhythm Movement

Put on some drum music. I like Gabrielle Roth's 5Rhythms (www.5rhythms.com) for dancing, but any music with a strong beat will work. Try Babatunde Olatunji for Nigerian percussion, Hamdi El-Khayyat or Movses Panossian's "Drum Circle" CD for an Arabian rhythm. Whatever you choose, turn it up loud and dance. Stomp the earth with the beat. Let the focus be on the rhythm of the music, not any specific dance move. It doesn't matter how you look. It only matters how you feel. Let the drumming move you. You may wish to describe this experience in your journal.

15 | Set an Intention

You've likely had the experience of going to the grocery store, list in hand, prepared to get what you need for your dinner plans. You've also likely arrived at the grocery store without a list and simply wandered the aisles, selecting whatever sounds good in the moment for your body. Both scenarios have benefits. The list keeps you on track, moving efficiently aisle by aisle and paying attention to your budget. But when you look for only what you're seeking, you can miss out on many things. Wandering can allow for new food choices and help you tune in to what your body needs in the present moment. Both scenarios also have challenges. If you only get what's on the list, you may become trapped in rigidity and routine. You may miss the gems in aisle 4. If you wander, you may wind up with a cupboard full of Doritos and not enough ingredients to make anything nutritious.

If you are blocked, consider setting an intention for your practice. This is your metaphorical grocery list for the session. What do you need? Why are you selecting those ingredients? An intention can give you focus—something to hold loosely in your mind and body as you practice. That intention helps quiet your mind. It gets your pen moving or your fingers typing. It can keep you from getting frozen by too many choices.

An intention for a writing session may be connected to a plot challenge or a character arc. It may be a research question or a prewriting immersion. Another type of intention might be to write for thirty minutes or to explore a thematic question from a new lens. An intention gives you some structure within which to work. It can give you parameters to challenge and excite your mind.

DEEP INQUIRY PRACTICES

Image Intention

Stand in Tadasana (Mountain Pose) with your feet about hip-width apart. Relax your shoulders, jaw, and neck. Let your arms hang loosely at your sides. Close your eyes, and on an inhalation, reach your arms above your head with the intention of gathering your story from the air around you. The more specific you can be with your intention, the better your results will be. For example, "I want to gather imagery for the conflict scene between Bob and Mary." Make the intention specific to what you're working with. Bring your arms back down and place your palms across your lower belly, gathering the energy there. Hold for a few breaths. If you like, you can ground your meditation by slowly folding forward (don't lock your knees!) and pressing your palms to the floor. To close, return slowly to standing, releasing your palms and offering gratitude. Move into a free-writing session from here.

Create a Manifesto

Create a manifesto (or womanifesto) for your writing and/or for yourself as a writer. You could also create a manifesto for each work-in-progress. This is a concise way to pin down what really matters to you about your project or about writing. Manifestos are evolving documents. You may also want to do a visual manifesto as a collage or Pinterest board. When I was working on the philosophy for my company, Fierce Monkey Tribe, I created a Fierce Monkey-festo. It encompasses what I believe about writing and writers, and it really helped focus my approach to the business. It not only helped me determine what I wanted, it also helped me understand what I didn't want, which is equally valuable. I've included it here as an example since it's about writing. Maybe some of the elements will help spring-board you into your own manifesto.

Rise up and write the story that will change everything!
Writers are compassionate creators, bridge builders, paradigm

disrupters, heart openers, empathy warriors, magic makers, and sacred listeners.

Writers embody the secret weapons of empathy and humility, which, when combined with discipline, patience, and persistence, alchemize words into magic carpets.

When we respect and learn the craft of writing, we unleash its art.

Our talents transform into the tools we need to love and live deeply.

Writers ignite changes that help alleviate suffering on a personal and global level.

Writers do not isolate in ivory towers, throw words as stones, or hold stories hostage to victimize and brutalize others.

We are relevant and necessary.

Know this: The Stories need their Writers, and Writers need their Stories. Together, we can love the world alive.

16 | Build Trust

As our relationship with our writing deepens, it begins to nudge us ever deeper into ourselves and our work. It carts us along, and before we know it, we are somewhere we never intended to be. This surprise can make us pull up short. Contract. Resist. Where are we? We traveled so deep and far into the woods, and it was so lovely that we forgot to mark the trail. "Hey, Writing, I just followed you, and now I can't see where to go next. I can't see how to get back. Where did you disappear to?"

When you are disoriented and confused, you may feel like your trusted companion, your writing, has suddenly exited stage left. All that time you spent cultivating a relationship and now what? It's getting dark in the woods. Unfamiliar noises begin to buzz and hum. The temperature is dropping (or rising). Did you bring enough water? Food? Oh gosh, there's no Wi-Fi! Panic sets in, and you feel, as we are reminded in *Game of Thrones,* that the night is indeed "dark and full of shadows." Does anyone know where you are? Did you forget to leave a note? How long will it be before someone comes looking for you? Your feet won't move. Your stomach churns. The inside of your mouth turns to cotton. You'd better get out of this place. Click away. Google something. Check Facebook or your e-mail. Find a distraction that is familiar—that will deflect you from this discomfort. There must be a good cat video you can watch or some article you can get outraged about.

Wait, don't click away. The next time you find yourself in this "lost" place (and you will definitely find yourself back here if you're doing enough writing), say to yourself, "Wait. I've been here before. What if I stay awhile and see what happens?"

Have you ever gone into the woods for any period of time? If you sit still long enough, you begin to see things you previously overlooked. Where first you saw only the largest trees, as you remain still, you begin to see the leaves, acorns, and anthills. The longer you stay still and present, the more you see. The "hidden" begins to reveal itself to those who are patient and pay attention, those who, as the filmmaker Akira Kurosawa said, "dare not to avert their eyes." When you stay in your writing woods, where you once thought was nothing (emptiness) or only terrors, you'll soon find something else. You'll be able to see what the lost place itself is asking for and how you can help.

In a forest ecosystem, the lowest level—the level closest to the forest floor—is called the understory. How cool is that? Stay long enough in your writer's forest to find the understory of your own book. What's milling around there? What's waiting to share something with you? These unknown parts of the journey are where you transition from the author who is stuck to the author who is able to finish writing the book. These clearings and dark forests can occur multiple times in a project, so don't be alarmed. Continue to move forward even when you're not sure where you're going.

Writing changes us. Writers come to the page exploring questions, even if they don't know what those questions are at the beginning. The questions are the fuel for continued investment in the work. That question may have to do with our own lives, the lives of our ancestors, or the way we relate to the larger world. They may be questions about injustice, famine, poverty, or war. We don't have to know right away *why* we're writing what we're writing. The questions will reveal themselves because they are what keep things moving forward in the work. Questions, interestingly, are also what keep readers turning pages. No one else approaches the page with the same questions and wonder as you do. No one else can write your book because it lives only within you.

The Buddhist practice of Chöd teaches us that as we integrate our inner demons and fractured selves, we can heal those around us—not by actively going up to strangers and declaring them healed, but rather by the energetic repercussions of our own inner work rippling out into the larger world. If you've been writing for a long time, consider how you were changed by the writing of each project. Our work often provides a window into a world we haven't yet entered—or even believed we could enter. Writing dissolves old tethers and can propel us to the next space. But of course, to do that, we have to navigate the middle. We have to face the letting go of some things we no longer need. We have to risk not-knowing. Fortunately, our own writing can be our guide. If we have nurtured our relationship with our writing, we can feel confident trusting it when we can no longer see the way.

You may resist the familiarity of your own forest. You may worry that you've traveled this path too often. You may be frustrated to meet what you feel is the same question over and over again. But remember, no matter how often you revisit a question or a theme, you will be coming at it just a bit differently, from a different angle, a different depth, a different perspective. My dad died when I was nineteen, and I spent many years trying to deny that it happened and who I had to become to live in the reality of his being gone. When I returned to my writing, it was weak. I felt like I was writing the same thing over and over, and that it was perpetually sappy. I was an immature writer, and I wrote for product. "I'm going to write a *story*," I would say. It wasn't a practice or a process. I didn't yet understand that art is constantly practiced but never finished. That a skill never runs out of things it can teach us. Over many subsequent decades, I've learned that it's impossible not to write what is in us to write *and* that it is pointless to try to avoid where our work is taking us.

DEEP INQUIRY PRACTICES

Building Your Understory

Each day we show up for our writing, we're stabilizing its foundation. We're building a root system that will bring us nourishment from places we can't yet reach. Here are some good Inner Journal grounding and centering questions to ask throughout a project:

> » **Why does this project matter to me?** Note that the "to me" is very important. You can't know how your work will affect the

world, but you can consistently revisit how a project affects you. Why are you working on it? The responses can vary from day to day. This question can be a door into the transformation toward which the work is leading you.

» **What is the writing asking of me?** The sculptor David Esterly, in his book *The Lost Carving: A Journey to the Heart of Making*, wrote about his relationship with finding and getting to know the right piece of wood for the sculpture he is working on. He inquires each day what the wood is asking of him. Where is it taking him? What does it need him to know?

» **What do I have to surrender or release to fully experience all this writing session or project has to teach me?** In other words, what must shift so you can evolve into the person who will be able to finish the book? A sculptor can collect tools and wood, and retreat to the studio. We can collect our paper and pens, but our tools—our words and sentences—must also be conjured before we can shape them into a form for others. We have to create the wood before we make the first cut. Drafting is how we do that.

17 | Be Kind to Your Writing

We tend to be very uncomfortable when we don't understand something. It's human nature. Not knowing makes us feel vulnerable. As writers, we spend many hours, days, and months in not-knowing. Our work's deepest heart is revealed to us slowly, through committed practice and patience. I've tried many different ways to help my students become more comfortable with vulnerability. They want so badly to "get it." They want to be masters of their work, commanders of their ships. I understand, I really do, but I have to somehow convince them that not only is it OK, it's essential to not know everything all at once. When we feel vulnerable or uncomfortable, we can anger more easily and lash out at ourselves and our work. This will increase the tension in our bodies and minds and can contribute to a block.

One semester, my beautiful, normally mild-mannered students turned vicious when speaking about their own works-in-progress. It was as if a tiny evil creature slipped out of each of their mouths wielding Wolverine-like knives to cut down everything in its path before it had a chance to grow. Where did this venom come from? And what purpose might it serve if we could look within it? What lives within the bully? This class used words like *drivel, failure, garbage, crap, ridiculous, absurd,* and on and on to describe their early drafts. Mind you, they did not speak about their classmates' work in those terms. They reserved those labels for their own still-wriggling drafts. They treated themselves and their own creations worse than they would ever dream of treating another's work. At first, I pointed out what they were doing, but that didn't stop the behavior, so I tried an experiment.

I went to the dollar store and bought a bushel of brightly colored, stuffed, hanging monkeys—the kind with Velcro on their paws so they can hang from shelves. I took the monkeys to class and gave one to each student. "This monkey is your writing," I said. "It's your early draft. It's your beautiful creation." They looked at me like I was crazy, but I was used to that. "Go ahead," I continued. "Say mean things to it. Tell it it's worthless. Stupid. Drivel. It'll never amount to a decent monkey." And they tried, but of course they ended up laughing because they were fully grown adults being asked to yell at neon stuffed monkeys. It was absurd, right?

I'd hold each monkey's head, pressing down on the forehead to make it look sad when the student yelled at it. The class members started to understand what they were doing. They were destroying something precious with their words. Something new. Something still in the process of becoming.

No one is so intentionally mean that they'll slice down new creatures on purpose. They didn't realize the effects of their language on their creative process and their writing lives. They didn't know what unconscious damage they were doing to their own growth as artists.

When they could personify their work, which I encouraged them to refer to as "baby story monkeys" to help reinforce the vulnerability of this new relationship, they could begin to enter into a more mature place with the work. They could allow it to be whatever it was as it moved toward becoming what it would be. Personification of the draft itself allowed them to understand that early drafts and final drafts cannot exist within the same form. As long as they judged their work from its first breath, the work could never trust them enough to take the necessary risks to evolve into its future. Becoming is a fragile thing. We have to hold our work gently so we don't snuff out its life.

I was also interested in what was underneath their venom toward their work. What purpose did it serve? What was the teacher hidden in the bully's words?

I think we all have some degree of an insidious type of arrogance that erroneously convinces us that we are perfect, are never going to make that mistake, and are the lone superstar in the group. That arrogance also sneaks in masquerading as negative self-talk. If it can convince us we're not good enough in the beginning, then we'll never have to face the reality of our human fallibility. We'll avoid the risks necessary to grow.

Whichever manifestation this arrogance takes in a writer, underneath it lives fear. Fear of not being able to write the story that comes to us. Fear of not having the discipline or persistence or patience to finish. Fear of what might be possible. Fear of the amount of work involved. Fear of being seen, of speaking a truth, of being human. If we can cut down something before it has a chance to mature, then we can assure ourselves, through the magic of the self-fulfilling prophecy, that we'll never have to deal with what could have been. Strike first. Assume the power position, and eliminate uncertainty, vulnerability, and mystery—three elements, as it turns out, that are nonnegotiable in the creative process. Avoid meeting them, and you avoid everything.

DEEP INQUIRY PRACTICES

Furry Friends

Find a cute stuffed creature that you can use as a physical manifestation of your writing. Name it. Put it in your writing space. Be OK with the necessary childlike play involved in creation. Be OK with wonder. When you feel the urge to tear your work down and minimize its existence, look into the eyes of your stuffed friend, and whisper something loving to it instead.

Personify It

Create a personification of your writing. *This is a fluid activity. Your writing may appear differently to you from day to day. Don't get attached to one particular image or character.* Approach this as you would approach creating a character for your novel. Your writing doesn't have to embody a human form. It could be a raven. A scorpion. A triangle. Ask it for a name. Is there a texture? A sound? Where does it live? Can you describe its bedroom? Its backyard? How did it find you out of all the other writers in the world? Why is *this* writing *your* writing? Create a backstory for it. Consider a monologue, from your writing's point of view, beginning with, "I have to tell you . . ."

Writer's Inner Smile

This practice is a foundational Taoist practice. It is a relaxation technique as well as a heart-opening practice. We writers can use it to cultivate self-compassion, soothe our inner critic, and soften the negative self-talk that may build up over the long term with our writing practice. As you might suppose, trying to write well with a closed heart and a tense mind is quite difficult.

Using active imagination, envision your writing or current work-in-progress sitting across from you. It is smiling beautifully and completely at you. The smile radiates unconditional love and acceptance. Bring a slight smile to your own lips; draw your attention to the center of your forehead, between your eyebrows, and spiral the energy from the smile there. Smile to your thymus gland and heart. Smile to all your organs (lungs, liver, pancreas, spleen, kidneys, sexual organs, and reproductive system). Offer gratitude for their work. Continue carrying the smile from your writing or your work-in-progress down your intestinal tract (through your esophagus, stomach, small intestine, large intestine, bladder, and urethra). Return your inner gaze to the writing or work-in-progress smiling at you and gather in its energy again, this time sending the smile to your brain; the pituitary, thalamus, and pineal glands; and finally down your spinal column. Inhale deeply, and on the exhalation, gather all this energy in at your navel, or center, in the lower *dantian*. Stay here as long as you like, basking in the love your work and your writing have for you and your own inner compassion for yourself.

This activity can help you remember why you write and why you're writing the particular project you're currently working on. It can help decrease anxiety and resentment you may be feeling toward your work at any given point in the writing process, and it can be a much-needed interrupter in your self-judgment of your work.

18 | Follow Your Curiosity

Perhaps the most misunderstood and misinterpreted writing myth is "Write what you know." Its intentions are good. It's cautioning you not to make yourself look foolish by writing a scene that takes place in a world-class hospital surgery theater from the perspective of the anesthesiologist if you have not done due diligence researching that setting and those skills. It doesn't mean you can never write about a surgical procedure if you've never done one. You just need to do your research. If all of our characters and settings were taken from what we've directly experienced, how dull would literature be? But if you're going to set your story in the Bronx, visit it; if you can't visit it, Google Earth the heck out of it, read about it, and get your geography right.

I bring up this myth in connection to writer's block for two reasons. First, when taken literally, it can shut down imaginative leaps that need to occur—especially in early drafts. If we self-censor where our story is going too early in the process, it will never find its way. We authors have only lived our singular lives in our own bodies, genders, and social systems, but our books are populated with so many more. Second, even when taken at its essence, the myth can cause a strange writer's disease I call Obsessive-Compulsive Researchitis (OCR). This almost manic compulsion leads you to research every last detail about cooking procedures in the eleventh century to avoid that Amazon comment that slays you for using the wrong kind of seasoning in your medieval paranormal urban fantasy novel. Research is awesome, and never has it been easier. The world's knowledge is at our fingertips now. Perhaps it was a bit more difficult to research compulsively when we had to go to the actual library, pull the cards out of the card catalogs, wander around until we found what we were looking for, take it back to the table, read it, make notes, and return the material. That was a commitment. We had to focus on what we really needed to understand. Now, with a click, we're linked up to source after source. There's always something else to find out. And that is quite true. There *is* always something else to find out. How about that? Beware of research as distraction. Because many of us use our computers for both research and writing, research can feel deceptively like doing the writing. And while it's part of the necessary work of writing a book, it's *not* writing the book. We need to be sure we understand the difference.

Instead of "Write what you know," try "Write what you're curious about." A story is not a subway stop or a character's occupation. A story is about questions. It's about characters who have dilemmas (unsolvable problems), and those dilemmas become dramatized through story points. The dilemmas represent a myriad of questions that help lead the characters toward transformation.

A plot is not a story. A setting is not a story. A character arc is not a story. A story is thematic. It's *about* something. The "about" is the theme, and that theme is connected to the essential questions a piece is working through. Note that often in fiction, as in life, there are no answers at all. There are simply deeper perspectives or shifts in levels of understanding. Even nonfiction—perhaps with the exception of how-to-build-your-deck kinds of books—rarely provides definitive answers. Nonfiction also explores questions and presents arguments on various sides of a question. The word *essay*, in fact, means "to explore and test out."

The questions a book explores need to be of interest to the writer. If they aren't, there won't be enough fuel to keep the writing moving. If the writer could care less about the central theme of the book, then that apathy will come out in the writing, assuming the book ever gets completed. It's these questions that make fiction deeply personal to the author. We explore things that matter profoundly to us, even if we're using shape-shifters to enact the story.

For example, Toni Morrison's Pulitzer Prize–winning book, *Beloved*, may be set after the American Civil War in Ohio, but it is *about* slavery, race relations, and maternal love. It's about why (and there is no answer) one race decided it was superior to another and thus enslaved a people. It's about the nature of power and freedom and, above all, love. A mother is willing to kill her child rather than have her grow up a slave. Those are some serious stakes leading to a rash of unanswerable questions. As authors, we are drawn to explore some questions and themes, and we're not as interested in others. That's why thematic story questions are deeply connected to the writer. Morrison did not live in nineteenth-century Ohio, but she was affected enough by those questions of race, power, and love that she devoted herself to them, not just in this book but throughout her whole body of work. She keeps turning these questions over and over as if they were rocks in a tumbler, polishing a new gem each time.

In case you didn't get the memo, it takes a long time to write a book. It's not a Sunday afternoon project, no matter what some programs promise. If we are not interested in our story's questions, we won't make the time to show up to work through them. We won't have enough fire to keep the necessary enthusiasm. The questions—the curiosity—are the fuel for our journey. If you already know the answer, there's little left to say.

You may remember learning about thesis statements in high school English classes. A thesis statement can't be a fact, such as the earth revolves around the sun. When you state a fact, there's nothing left to explore. A strong thesis statement leaves room for a stance, a perspective, a new approach to a question. Writing is one way we help make sense of the world for ourselves, and then readers turn to our books to help make sense of their own chaotic and random world. As we write, our work sends up "trial balloons" during the drafting process. These balloons offer new ideas, other paths, and different insights about the work. Our work whispers clues to us, and we follow because that's what writers do.

An interesting phenomenon happens when you write. The act of writing itself changes you. You don't have to try to use writing as a therapeutic process for this to happen. You're simply not the same person at the end of a book. Your writing of it, your exploration of the questions, has shown you something. It's revealed an aspect of your self and/or taught you something. You experience a shift through the writing process, and the shift that occurs is the Mack truck you didn't see coming. It's the thing that smacks you senseless. Did it get your attention? Great. That was its job. Now that you're awake and paying attention, the deeper work can occur.

The writing you produce reveals something about you and something that can shift the perspectives of others who read it. But *how* you produce that work, the ways you show up or don't, the way you, warrior-like, meet your writing, reveals volumes about what makes you, you. Writing doesn't just show you the stories you share with the world. It isn't only a brand or a platform, or a carefully crafted persona. It shows you the stories you believe about yourself and the world, and when one of those stories becomes apparent, it can leave you undone. It can push you away from your work. It can pull back your veil for a moment and give you a glimpse of your authentic self looking right back. Well. Isn't that person something?

DEEP INQUIRY PRACTICE

Gather Your Questions

What questions are you currently exploring in your life? Are you dealing with empty nest syndrome? A breakup? A new job? Health issues? What's on your mind? Do you see any connection to the questions in your life and the questions within your writing project? It can help to think of fiction as a stage for these explorations. The heart of any piece of writing has a link to the heart of the writer. We simply couldn't do the work without that connection. Do we sit down to write and say, "Gosh, I'm ready for some serious transformation? I'm ready to explore all the hidden things I possibly can." Not likely. Depending on the kind of writer you are and your natural process, you may first hear a character's whisper. You may be captivated by an abandoned building and begin with the question, "What happened here?" You may have an image or a sound that you can't shake, so you follow its trail. Write *into* what haunts you. Write what you don't yet understand. (But yes, if you're setting it in the Bronx, get your train schedules right!)

19 | Recognize the Characteristics
of the Stages

Why do questions matter so much to a story? Because they *move*. An answer is a stop. A question gets you and your story out of bed and into the day ahead. Questions are open doors. They move you away from the stagnation of certainty into the openness of wonder. Questions stretch you. They challenge and confound you. They shake you up, rock your world, shimmy your shins. They propel you to the next place. Answers are not the point of questions unless the answer you find stretches you further and pulls you into even deeper questions. Let the answers you uncover be the scaffolding as you leap from question to question. Don't let them be quicksand that holds you still, eventually drowning you. Let's briefly discuss the various kinds of questions we tend to associate with different parts of both our stories and our writing practice.

The Beginning: Potential and Promise

In the beginning, the potential you see for both yourself as a writer and your work is vast. The promise is limitless. You can be anything. Write anything. Your unwritten book can be the Best Thing Ever Written. When everything is possible, then nothing is impossible. All is open space. Who showed up to populate your book? What is it about? What could the book's future hold? A Pulitzer? A National Book Award? It can be everything because *it has not yet been anything*.

When you move into the work more deeply, you start to realize that everything you imagined is not possible because your story simply must have a focus if it is to be comprehensible. It cannot be all things because "everything" translates into nothing on the page. You must select what you will let in and what you will keep out. As you realize you can't create what you first imagined, you may question your ability to make craft-based, story-focused, intuitive choices and come face-to-face with your own version of the inner critic as you leave the sunny shores of beginning and enter the storm. "I thought I knew what to do, but now I don't" is a common refrain as the beginning yields to its natural middle.

The Middle: Tension and Chaos

It all seemed easy and doable in the beginning. We would jaunt forth into an adventure, sure the fates were with us, and there would be no unexpected roadblocks. As we were compiling our playlist for this grand road trip, something sneaky happened. We ran into trouble. External and internal trouble. The middle is about uncertainty. What do we do next? What will happen? How in the name of everything can we get our protagonist out of this mess? Uncertainty creates anxiety, and anxiety manifests in both internal and external ways for the writer. In a story, the middle is where everything that used to work stops working.

The End: Reframes and Transformation

Our hero (or you as the writer) has moved through the chaos and is changed by the journey. Now the fire that propelled the original desire and the beginning questions has alchemized into something new. There's an ease now within the book and your journey. It's a time to rest. The questions of an ending are reflective: "Where have I been? How have I changed? What (if any) meaning can be made of the choices and actions I made along the way?"

Understanding the nature of your questions and where they might fall in the stages of your project or process can help normalize your feelings about where you are. Questions can also provide you with built-in prompts to springboard yourself out of a block and back into the story. Take a look at the stage you're in within your book. Beginning? Middle? End? What are the natural questions of those places? You can use them to kick-start a journal entry. Understanding where you are in the book's process or your own development can also help you see the larger continuum of work and keep you from getting myopic about one particular writing session or story problem.

DEEP INQUIRY PRACTICE

State-of-the-Book Touchstone

Replace the word *book* with whatever you're currently working on— state of the poem, essay, memoir, graphic novel. Then take time to consider where you are and where you want to be. This exploratory exercise will help you take stock. Use this touchstone throughout your writing process whenever you feel the need to regroup and reground yourself in your work. Use these Inner Journal questions as guideposts:

» What did the last thing I wrote reveal to me?
» What are the larger questions my work is evoking?
» If I'm stuck, where do I feel that resistance in my body?
» What's the one thing I'm sure this work is not about?
» If I am holding anything back, who am I afraid will read it? Why?
» What's the final image of this work?
» What's the feeling I want readers to have when they finish my book?
» What are two options for starting places in my next writing session?

Feel free to modify the questions and create your own. This is also an exercise in nonjudgment. Don't beat yourself up over what you haven't done or measure what you've done against what you thought it could be. This is a chance to look cleanly and with compassionate detachment at your current state of affairs. This is not the time to tear things down or slip into spirals of shame. Meet your work where it is and say hello.

20 | Learn to Spot Impending Transitions

My colleague Jeffrey Davis refers to the middle places as times of "fertile confusion." I really like this term, both because it has a positive connotation and because it encompasses seemingly opposing elements—fertility and confusion—into a single concept. The times when we are thrown off guard are times of great potential. Rather than run from them because we don't yet have (or think we have) the tools to navigate this strange new world, what if we moved into our middle passages with curiosity and trust, with excitement for what may come next?

Just as it is within our writing process, the middle of a narrative is where the old way of thinking comes crashing into the need for a new way of thinking for our protagonist. We haven't yet moved into the new way of thinking, but we can see its shimmering necessity just over the horizon. It's where the defense mechanisms, old patterns, and old belief systems start to fail our noble hero. It's where *if* our protagonist is really committed to his goal, something needs to change, and there's no longer any denying it. The goal of the protagonist can also shift here. Maybe he doesn't want what he thought he wanted after all, but as a result of this crashing together of belief systems, he sees something new. Chaos ensues in the attempt to find the next right steps. Anything can happen. With this new dawning awareness, choices must be made to keep momentum. The next step our hero takes is vital to achieving the new goal. No wonder there's so much anxiety, so much tension here! If the author has written the middle effectively, the reader won't be able to put the book down until she finds out what happens next. So high are the stakes. So great is the hero's risk to transform.

The stakes are so high in the middle of narrative, the choices so many, that it's easy to get overwhelmed. Sometimes that overwhelmed feeling manifests as boredom. You think you know your story. You're sick to death of it. You just want the protagonist to get to the end already so you can move on to something else. You're itchy. You're uncomfortable. You choose the first possible way out of the tension in the middle just to move along. Or you grow weary of your own voice, your characters, your themes. You forget why you were drawn to them, and you find little value in them. You're bored. Feeling bored is one of those signals to pay deeper attention. Boredom is trying to tempt you away from your desk and into something new and splashy. It is part of the process. Wait it out.

It's sometimes said that plot in fiction is simply life with all the boring parts cut out. That's not quite accurate, because plot has an inherent causal relationship, but the second part—eliminating the boring parts—certainly holds true. When I was a girl, I couldn't figure out why characters in books never went to the bathroom or washed dishes or did anything *ordinary.* I can now see that those activities are rarely relevant to the dramatic question of the book, but at the time, it just seemed odd. I thought I was reading about someone's actual life. But of course, what I was reading were the relevant scenes that would dramatize the transformational and defining moments in the character's world.

In actual life, however, we are compelled to do many activities that aren't dramatically interesting. We do laundry. We pick up the kids. We brush our teeth. We mow the lawn and vacuum the floors. These things can seem tedious because we don't always see how they're relevant to our larger dramatic questions—our hopes and dreams for our lives. Think of a soap opera (you know you've watched at least one!). Nothing in a soap opera is mundane. If someone is nursing a sick child, it's because that child is seconds from death, or the mother is really the lost twin sister of the town's evil yet beautiful and wealthy matriarch. To keep viewers coming back, soap operas keep characters in high-stakes chaos most of the time. There can be a few episodes of calm (the lovers finally get together), but soon enough that becomes boring and some new threat is introduced to the narrative. Soap operas are focused on the parts of a story a viewer can't turn away from and rightly so. But between those events lies everything else—the grocery lists, the silences, the bad-hair days, the no-money months. Those events, rarely dramatized in stories, are the very things that connect a life over time.

So all this means is that boredom is normal. When you're writing a long project, you're going to reach not only the chaos but the boredom. Who cares? Not even you. It's part of the deal. Dust a few shelves and keep going.

None of us are the same. The following examples of signals of impending transitions may not be applicable to you. Feel free to add your own. Remember, just as we discussed with perfectionism and procrastination, it's less about the actual pattern, which is neutral, than about the meaning you give the pattern and the purpose for which you use it. A glass of wine is not a problem. Unless it is. Everything is contextual. That said, here are some common signals that a transition is on its way:

» Resistance to your writing practice or your work itself. This is hands down the most common behavior I've observed in myself and my students.

» A perpetual need to start the book over. (Yes, there is really a benefit to writing a draft through to the end before revision.)

» Physiological changes before you start your writing practice, such as sore muscles, an upset stomach, or sleep disruptions.

» Negative self-talk, such as, "I can't do this," "I'm a terrible writer," or "This is a waste of time."

» Jealousy over other writers' successes. This is frequently a transference of your frustration toward your work onto others. Look for thoughts like, "They never publish anyone good anymore. There's no respect for 'real' writers these days. That best-selling mega-author is a hack. Look at those adverbs in the book!"

» New projectitis. You start a new book every time an old one gets difficult.

» Time stuffing. You figure out ways to overschedule yourself so there is simply "no time" to write.

» Confusion over the narrative direction of the story—a befuddled plot, character development snags, and so on.

» Resentment of the characters in your work.

» Feelings that everything you've ever written is garbage.

» Agitation, anger, and uncharacteristic behavior toward others.

Notice that some of these items don't relate directly to writing but rather to how the writer relates to the world. That's because your relationship with your writing is part of your makeup. You can't cordon it off from everything else you do. Because humans are masters at deflection and projection, if you start to observe behavior in other areas of your life that aren't typical for you, you may want to look at how things are going with your writing and see what it may be trying to tell you.

As you become more aware of your tendencies and patterns, when you sense that a transition may be just around the corner and your writing may be about to show you something unexpected, first take a breath and offer gratitude for noticing the possibility. Then try one of the following Deep Inquiry Practices to keep you from turning your back on everything and taking up underwater basket weaving.

DEEP INQUIRY PRACTICES

Change It Up

Step out of your current writing routine for a week. Don't work on the current project at all. We're not machines, and we cannot produce the same output from day to day. *However,* instead of just walking away for the week, each morning and each evening, either whisper "Hello" to your writing in the morning and "Good night" when you go to bed, or write the words down on paper. That's it. You're maintaining contact with the work, but you're not forcing yourself to address something that isn't quite working right now. You're just letting your work know you haven't abandoned it. You're taking care of your own needs for a while.

Sometimes, we need to change things up. Try writing in a different location or at a different time. If you usually write on a computer, try doing it by hand. Read a book you've been saving. Go see a film or a play. Go for a hike. Watch the cloud formations. Listen to music. Go to the zoo. It doesn't matter what you do—just make it something different.

Leave Your Writing a Voicemail

Record a conversation with your writing. You can use an app like Audio Memos or any handheld recorder. This isn't about the sound quality. Just turn it on and start talking: "Hey there. I wanted to check in with you." Ramble on as much as you like. You can speak directly to your writing or to the work-in-progress. Don't listen to the recording right away. Wait a few days and then listen to what you had to say. You can reverse this as well and speak *as* your writing or work-in-progress talking to you. Don't forget to press Record! It's nearly impossible to remember what you said. It's best to just do a voice recording here rather than using your computer's camera to record yourself as well. It's too easy to be distracted by your own image as you speak.

Invite It In

Create an invitation, either on the computer or with actual paper and pen, welcoming whatever is approaching. You're essentially saying to your work, "It's OK. I'm making a space for you. Please come visit."

Dress It Up

Create a visual collage or other type of representation for what has occurred in your work-in-progress up till now. You can do this on the computer or the old-fashioned way with glue, magazine pictures, and poster board. Find photographs, words, images—anything that connects to where your current work has been. Then create a second collage that represents what you envision for the next leg of the project's journey. What do you think is going to happen next? What are some images that represent the transformations your primary characters must go through? Any phrases or words that call to you from the other side? If you have a Pinterest account, you may want to create Pinterest boards for the two collages. Pinterest allows you to make boards private if you don't want to share.

Create a visual collage or Pinterest board for the blocked part itself. Anything is fair game here. What does this place feel like right now, and what images represent those feelings? You might want to pick one of your characters and explore what he or she is feeling at the moment through images and phrases.

21 | Move into Transitions

The middle is a transition point, and transitions, of course, are changes—most people's absolute favorite things to do! As we've talked about, a writing project requires writers to change, and even though most people experience some discomfort around change, the changes frequently yield something better. Consider the American myth of reinvention—a cornerstone of America's worldview. It is based on the premise that there is always the potential for change. A chance to do something different. A new beginning. A clean slate. This is a highly seductive mythology, and like most myths, it can be beneficial or toxic depending on how it's implemented. It is amazing to be on the threshold of something fresh, to reinvent. It's also a luxury. The poet and teacher Hiro Boga, speaking on transitions, writes about the "sizzle between here and there." Transitions are electric, alive. For change to occur, something must be released to make room for what's coming.

Here's a low-stakes example. I love clothes. I love the way they feel. The way different colors and textures splash into one another and create art. The way trying on a jacket or pants with a new cut can change—not me, but the *potential* for me. Oh, how intoxicating (and debt-inducing if I don't pay attention)! I enjoy imagining who I could be in a certain outfit, a certain heel height. Could I be a person who wears a Chanel suit? How about a biker vest? The one time I tried on stilettos in a store, I almost broke an ankle, so I'm probably not the person who could walk around Manhattan in those shoes, but maybe I could be if . . . This imagining is fun for me, a dabbling in the potential path game. All the lives I could still choose spread out in front of me. But the stakes are low as I meander through my small town's stores. Whether I buy anything or not, I'm going home to the same townhouse, the same cats, the same husband. I'm going to work at the same college. The clothes let me change external skins for a day or two, and they could be a catalyst for a deeper change, but most of the time, they're just fun. They're fun for me precisely because the rest of my life is stable. What if I had to buy that Chanel suit because I was starting a new job in a new field in a new city? The stakes just got significantly higher. Suddenly that suit—nothing more than cloth and thread—is carrying a great deal of expectation. Real transitions, the ones with real stakes and real consequences, aren't as easily navigated by the perfect designer.

Here's an example with far higher stakes. The Grand Canyon climber, river guide, and archaeologist Scott Thybony creates a series for our local NPR station called "Grand Canyon Commentaries." In his July 3, 2014, broadcast, he talked of his own experience as an avid and skilled Grand Canyon hiker when he once found himself literally stuck on a cliff face, unable to move up or down. He had been following a passage cut through the inner gorge by Hance Creek. When he reached a pour-off, he turned back to try and find a bypass around the drop. He discovered two options. One was a climb up hundreds of feet of talus. The other was a shorter climb up broken Vishnu schist. He chose the shorter climb, and when he was fifty feet above the streambed, he realized he'd made a terrible mistake. It was too dangerous to keep climbing, but it was also too risky to turn back. He hung there on the face of the cliff, immobile inside and out. He knew he had to take some action—up or down—before his muscles tired and he fell. He slowly began inching his way back down, millimeter by millimeter until he reached the creek bed.

For a successful life transition to occur, we must let something go. We can't choose both. Thybony couldn't go up and down; he had to choose. We can't cart everything with us to that next place—whether it's a spouse, a job, a home, an idea, a dream—something must be surrendered. Otherwise, the weight of what we bring with us will keep us from making it to the next place. Too often, we try to move into the next thing carrying every stitch of our old skins with us. Not because we aren't convinced of the need to make a change or because we believe everything is currently working perfectly, but because the place between the old and new is so raw. So vulnerable. So full of sizzle. It's natural to want to carry that old skin with us for protection until we get a sense of our new environment's landscape. But life is funny and doesn't seem to want to let us do that. To make a complete transition, we have to shed what can't come with us. Writing a book takes us through a life transition. It asks us to release what we can't take with us.

Let's consider the breath. We inhale oxygen and exhale carbon dioxide. But it's really at the peak of that breath—when the inhalation is completed and the exhalation hasn't yet begun—that the transformation occurs. This is when the breath is changed from something that nourishes us to something we no longer need—the bonus is that the thing we're releasing nourishes other life-forms. We can't keep inhaling forever. Everyone understands that. But when we look at many other areas of life, it seems like we might be able to keep gathering things forever without letting anything go. We take in and take in and take in, and it becomes increasingly difficult to know what to release. How can we know what we will no longer need when we've already needed so much? To complicate matters further, the things we've carried with us from experience to experience now carry the weight of all the dreams and expectations we had for the life of which those items were a part. What a huge risk there is in letting go. Let's take it and see what happens.

DEEP INQUIRY PRACTICES

Transition Breath Meditation

Find a comfortable, quiet place. You can sit or stand. If you're sitting in a chair, make sure your feet rest flat on the floor. If you're seated on the floor, make sure your hips are above your knees, placing a cushion underneath you, if necessary. If you're standing, place your feet slightly more than hip-width apart. Relax your knees and sink your weight into your feet. No matter what position you're in, connect with the energy of the earth through the soles of your feet or the backs of your legs and thighs. Take a few deep breaths to settle yourself. Relax your jaw and tongue. Draw your shoulders up to your ears and release them down your back.

Inhale slowly to a count of four. At the top of the inhalation, hold the breath for a count of four. Exhale on another count of four. Practice three rounds of this breath before returning to your normal breathing pattern.

If you'd like to practice this breath with a meditation, here's one to try: On the inhalation, say to yourself, "I am gathering in what I need." While you hold the breath, say to yourself, "I am sorting through what I have." And on the exhalation, say to yourself, "I am releasing what I do not need."

After you've completed the breathing practice, try free-writing in your journal for fifteen minutes. If you need some prompts to help you get started, try these:

» Before the leap, I . . .
» During the leap, I . . .
» After the leap, I . . .

Transition Junction

Explore these Inner Journal questions when you feel blocked:

» What is behind me? In other words, what have I already written? This isn't necessarily about the plot, but more about the themes.
» Where did you come from? (You can ask this question of the book, of yourself, or of a character in your work.)
» What do I feel grateful for about what I have already written?
» What do I see when I look into the abyss in front of me? What images come? What words?
» What is the question(s) of the next step? What characters, settings, conflicts are there to help me write into that question?

» What were the significant scenes, characters, and/or questions of what I've already written? What might those questions reveal about what is still to come?

» Envision the next line of dialogue in your book. Write it. Then inquire into the essential nature of what came before that line was uttered.

22 | Find Your Storyverse

I spend a lot of time thinking about what exactly writers do. Countless books talk about craft, as if we were *only* constructors—assemblers of disparate elements. Still more books attempt to discuss the ever and always elusive muse, the thing that we all agree is something, somewhere, somehow, but what and where and how are impossible to agree on or quantify. There's some part of the writing process that is simply immeasurable. Talent, the muse, the source—many names attempting to name the nameless. For the sake of this conversation, I'm going to name this nameless part the Storyverse. This place (mythical? imaginary? crazy?) is where our writing lives—where the characters and stories, poems and essays swirl around waiting for the right writer to show up and build them a bridge to our world, word by word. If you think that's too crazy to keep reading, then I encourage you to come up with your own place where your writing hangs out. Personify it and create its space.

For me, the Storyverse circles the planet—a layer of the atmosphere that's invisible to all scientific equipment. I get access to a small part of it through my work. I find my stories and characters there. I'm not exactly sure how, but over thirty years of writing seriously, I know it happens.

When I was a girl, I would sit in bed and line up all my stuffed animals in a ring around me. Each animal had a name, a backstory, and a reason for being in the circle that night. Each of them was going to have a special mission while I slept. I mostly had cats and bears and bunnies. The cats were always in charge of dreams; the bears were supposed to keep out the ghosts; and the bunnies were swift of foot, able to run and get help if necessary. I loved the dark, but I knew it was full of things I couldn't see. Things that somehow made me who I was. I spent a lot of time alone, but that wasn't a problem. I had books, I had my animals, and I had their stories. I could go anywhere with those three things. I could be anyone.

As I grew older and had to face middle school, I quickly learned that the very things that made me feel safe and excited to be alive were liabilities on the mean streets of prepubescent life. In fifth grade, I carried yarn animals that I made from my mother's abandoned knitting projects in a small plastic barrel. I kept them in my desk, and when I felt anxious, I would press my hand against its cool surface. One day, the inevitable happened. The mean girls found out about my yarn monkeys and giraffes and cats, and they teamed up with the mean boys. Since I was about as good a fighter as I was an athlete, it was easy for them to grab the barrel from my desk. They tossed it back and forth. The teacher, as usual, was out of the room. I didn't know what to do, but I remember their laughter, how it felt hot and hollow in my belly. I remember feeling anchored to my chair, powerless as the children emptied my animal friends across the desks, their wide googly eyes searching for me to help them as they'd always helped me. But I couldn't move. Those kids—the sneers on their lips, the slick of their spit—froze me. Eventually the teacher returned. The bullies, like shadows, slipped into their chairs, and if I hadn't seen the red and blue arm of my monkey sticking out from between the desks, even I would have wondered if it had happened at all. I gathered my friends back up, put them in the barrel, and locked it in my lunch box. I could feel them shivering.

This is how writing and my role as a writer have felt for me. When I was ten, I was accused of being too sensitive, too childish, too in-the-clouds. But really, who would have wanted to be on the ground in that room with those children? Forty years later, I'd still choose yarn animals over them. Forty years later, I see what I was really responding to and why it mattered then and matters still. It wasn't the meanness of children, which is to be expected, and it wasn't the bullying, which as far as bullying goes was pretty run-of-the-mill. It wasn't even the violation of having my friends taken from me. It was the awareness that I had a palpable relationship with those creatures, which were only yarn and glue to the rest of the world. I'd infused them with personalities, struggles, and dreams. They had names. They shared their stories with me, it seemed at the time, only because I took a moment to listen. And because I'd heard their stories, I was invested in them in a way that was as real to me as human friendship. I had somehow taken on some responsibility for them because I'd heard their tales. I'd become a guardian, a caretaker, of some kind of energy that fed me. When I watched those yarn creatures spill out into the unsafe space of a fifth-grade classroom, I felt like I had broken a sacred trust. They had come to me. They brought their stories to me. And I just sat and watched while the world made fun of all that they were.

That was the beginning. The first forging of my soul in the world of writers. The first prick of awakening to who I am. As I grew up and middle school no longer mattered, I began to consider the idea that what made me weird was also what gave me my voice and my perspective as a writer. The things about me that were liabilities in childhood turned out to be my greatest strengths in adulthood. The ways I didn't fit in became the ways I stood out. Even though the world will always have bullies, and there will always be people who think I'm just weird (not in that good way!), I've learned that the more I embody my spark, the farther it will reach. The less I hide, the stronger I become.

Today, I can talk about the Storyverse with all the confidence in the world. I can see that the way I hear characters is unique to me and that I can help other writers with their unique ways of accessing their own worlds only if I can fully embody mine. Having a physical place, even if it is "only" imagined, gives me a place to step into when I write. It gives me a destination that is familiar, that changes as needed, reveals what is necessary, and withholds what I'm not yet ready to see. My Storyverse is my writing's GPS coordinates. It's an imaginative address. My animal friends from fifth grade came from its shelves. So did my puppets as I grew older. My first inklings of stories and poems. My first novel. My dreams. The voices I walked with when I was alone, and the ghosts that followed me when the dark came—they all had an address. Could I create a path that would take me there consistently? Sure! Why not? The part of me that I'd long kept hidden—the part of me that made others laugh at me or avoid me—was the source of all I am. Want to come inside? Maybe it'll inspire you to find your own Storyverse—your own never-ending source.

Laraine's Storyverse

When you come near my Storyverse, you'll almost miss it if you're not paying close attention. Like the mythical jinni's palace in the clouds, the Storyverse hides in plain sight. It's in the Deep South, surrounded by trees and swamps. The air is alive with sounds—tree frogs, crows, the scuttle of sand crabs—and thick with damp. You approach the base of the Storyverse quite by accident. It's a thick tree trunk, as wide as a train car, its roots poking up from beneath the red clay earth. If you look to the sky, you'll see the branches are even wider than the trunk, reaching to all cardinal directions. In its arms is a foundation. In front of you is a rope ladder. How could you have missed this?

You'll step back, and when you do, you'll see the three-story Gothic structure, two turrets on either side with copper spires winding into the thinner upper branches. The paint is a faded Carolina blue, the window-eyes long and thin, lidded with heavy velvet drapes. You move closer again, touch the thick rope. It's then that you notice the smell. Paper. Feral. Metallic. The rope hangs through a trapdoor. You climb one-two-three to the top and push. It opens upward, and when you poke your head through, still hanging tightly to the rope, you gasp. Three stories of bookcases line all the walls. Up, up, up, farther than you can see, are colorful spines of books. Some shake and shiver. Others are still. You push yourself up into the house, and the trapdoor closes behind you. The ladder is gone.

You are inside. Cats sleep on window seats. Black ones. Orange ones. White ones. One cat has wings, but you blink twice and it vanishes. Crows roost in the eaves. Butterflies open and close the book covers of their wings. Along the deep mahogany wood floors are card catalogs, the handles rubbed brown with years and years of finger touches. Two drawers are open, and you step closer. Images. A pinwheel. A dandelion. A kite. Summer 1953. A question rises within you. What does that mean? What is its significance?

The question takes root in you and starts to sprout chapters. Spiral staircases wind their way through the floors, getting narrower and narrower as you reach the top. On the uppermost floor, the moon and sun light opposite windows. On the lowest floor, the earth is freshly turned. The cemetery stones are newly carved. The names shift as you read. "Who is that?" you ask before it vanishes. "Why is she here?" The stones take root with the butterfly, grounding you and lifting you up. Handwritten notes spill out of the drawers of the card catalogs. Dates. Names. Places. Some you gather; others you leave for later. Sunset and sunrise compete for attention. The earth is dotted with glowworms, the earth's stars. When it's time to leave, you feel the living weight of your gifts—characters, settings, ideas—in your backpack. You close your eyes and whisper, "Thank you." The door opens. The ladder swings, and you step down three-two-one onto the ordinary world's soil.

I visit my Storyverse daily. I find my next steps there. I find my next books, and I catch glimpses of the ones I am close to but will never write. It's limitless yet contained by solid walls I can touch. I visit it for peace. For inspiration. For connection. For friendship and challenges. It is my source.

DEEP INQUIRY PRACTICE

Create Your Storyverse

Spend some time considering your own relationship to your writing's source and how it manifests for you. Describe it. Draw a picture of it, or find one online or in a magazine that you can post in your work area. When you know where it is, you can determine what kind of path you need to clear to get there. Use all of your imagination.

You may want to draw a door, a window, or a bridge that your writing uses to travel from its point of origin to the page. In what condition does it arrive? How do you greet it? Consider any textures or smells you may notice. Where does it reside when it isn't with you? Can you describe this place?

You're mining your active imagination with this activity. You're not worried about what's true (is there an actual Storyverse?). You're creating an environment—an entire ecosystem where you and your work can meet. When you create this (and the more specifically you do it the better), you are creating sacred space. You are concretizing what is invisible and creating a dimensional place that you can visit to access your creative flow. You'll be less likely to get discouraged and throw up your hands in frustration if you can be still and center yourself and have somewhere to go in your mind to find your work. You will also be triggering your imaginative flow simply by participating in this activity, so you'll be that much further along when you get to the page.

Consider the relational aspect between writer and writing in a more tangible way. Sometimes your writing won't be home, and that's fine. Just leave it a note. Let it know you made the trip.

Be flexible in this activity as you are with all the others. Your approach and location don't have to be anything at all like mine. Be aware as well that you can change it up, and if you do the meditation many times, you'll find different "rooms" for your work. Don't be attached to one room or space. Just pay attention. That's the heart of it all—attention. Energy follows intention. Be sure to send it where you want it to go.

23 | Let Your Writing Take the Lead

Have you ever noticed how a parent and infant communicate? There's a unique language that makes sense only for the two of them. Intimate partners also often develop some kind of personal vocabulary—a language that reflects the nature of their relationship. A language that, although English, may make no sense to an outsider. Maybe you have a secret language for speaking to your dog or cat. There are also specific languages associated with different businesses and industries—hospitals, education, retail, engineering. Your own job has its shorthand, and when employees of a particular company get together, their conversation is peppered with references and stories that only those employees will understand.

Your writing, believe it or not, has its own unique way of communicating with you, and it isn't in your native language—at least not in the way you think of it. Our writing leaves us trails of breadcrumbs every time we rise to meet it, but we don't recognize them until we learn to translate what it is saying into a format we can understand.

An obstacle in our path to understanding this intimate communication is our belief that we're always in charge of what ends up on the page. If you're resistant to letting go of your illusion of complete control over your work, I encourage you to go back and reread something you wrote when you felt you were "in the zone." How much did you remember of what you wrote? How often do you surprise yourself when you're writing? "Wow! This story is about *that*? Where did this character come from?" As you take writing more and more seriously, you'll start to have more of these "zone" experiences. It's not that you have nothing to do with what you craft; you have everything to do with it. It's in the *drafting* that the biggest hints and messages show up in your work. It's in the drafting that your writing takes the lead over your intellect. Let it. In this stage, the writing itself drops bread-crumbs for us to follow. The challenge is to understand its language and decipher its code.

Our connection to our art is a channel that is uniquely ours. Yes, there are millions of other writers in the world, but only you have your unique connection to your work. When you can cultivate an understanding with your own work, you will feel more empowered as a writer—not in a controlling way, but in a respectful and trusting way. You will see, through direct experience and process awareness, that there is always something of value in a writing session. Something is always offered up. You'll notice you can't always see the gift in the moment, but a disciplined practice will have shown you that, just like the erosion that creates new landscapes over time, things are always in motion, and when you're not looking, a wonder of the world appears.

DEEP INQUIRY PRACTICE

Panning for Gold in Your Draft

Over a long writing practice, we send ourselves signals about the work-in-progress. The days where nothing seems to be happening are actually helping us accumulate the keys to the larger soul of the work. Our role is to pay attention to these often-hidden clues. One way to gain perspective on where you are in your work is to explore each session through the lens of a miner panning for gold in the stream of your consciousness. I like to focus on imagery—the shiny parts—to start with. So much is contained within the image, and images are often direct links to our unconscious minds, the master behind the scenes of our creative work. When we review our work with an eye toward patterns, or what we're saying underneath the words, we can gain a great deal of insight that we may overlook if we're constantly criticizing our story arcs or our character development.

After a writing session, read quickly through the work you gener-ated. Do not—and this is very important—mark it up; scratch things out; rip out pages; or in any way critique the writing or how it fits in the larger project. You must practice nonjudgment and deep compassion for your work here. This is not a revision exercise. It is not an editing exercise. It's an exploratory exercise, and for it to be effective, you have to refrain from predetermining the worth of what you've just created. (Hopefully you can see how this will be helpful in your writing life overall!)

After you've read through the session without judgment or red pen in hand, on a new piece of paper or in a new document, create a quick list of images in the scene or chapter you're currently struggling with. Give yourself no more than two minutes to create the list. Then circle or highlight the image that is calling to you most strongly. Begin an inquiry process into that image to help you deepen and expand it. Draw the image if you like. Talk to the image. Here are some Inner Journal prompts to get you started:

1. What do you (the image) want?
2. What do you need?
3. What's something you're hiding that I can't see yet?
4. What do you need to tell me?
5. What is your texture?
6. What sounds surround you?
7. What do you need from the work?
8. How do you support the work?

You can practice this activity at any point in the writing process, from early drafts through revisions. Try it anytime you feel compelled to move deeper. Use it whenever you feel the writing hadn't gone as far as it could have. It will help train you to spot the hidden clues living within all your writing sessions. It will help you not toss away the flickering jewels.

24 | Embrace the Middle

You know that moment in life when you realize you've got to back up and do something a little differently? That moment when you know you're making a mistake, but you're going to push forward just one more step because you can't bear to regroup and do what needs to be done? You know it's a misstep. You may feel it first in your belly. Maybe it's a twitch in your neck, a dryness in your mouth, or a shortness of breath. Even a whisper: "Hey, you. Yeah, I'm talking to you. It's time to learn something." And even though you're excited about learning and growing—you've been alive long enough to know that learning and growing tend to come with some kind of release—you know it's going to hurt more than a little bit. So you may resist.

When faced with unfamiliar ground and many different choices, it's easy for the mind to latch on to a belief about what this unfamiliar place is all about. The normal and natural block—the pause in the creative process—becomes something much larger than it is. When the belief is attached to the block, it doesn't take too long for that belief to become "the Truth."

Rather than think of the middle as a literal place, think of it as a state of mind for the writer. When I speak of *the middle* in this book, I'm not necessarily talking about the literal middle—page 125 in a 250-page manuscript. I'm referring to any point in your writing where you are transitioning from one way of being to another, one kind of reality to the next. This might happen to you on day three of your writing practice, or it may not happen until you're in draft four. It is an emotional and psychological space rather than a literal physical space.

For many of us, the middle can have negative connotations. For example, consider the work week. Wednesday, hump day, doesn't have the allure of a beginning (Monday) or the promise of a weekend (Friday). We know intuitively that Wednesday is a transition point, a day between the start and finish.

I also think about middle age, probably in part because I'm now unequivocally there. In middle age, we're redefining many things about ourselves. Kids are leaving home. Parents are aging and may need our care. Our bodies are starting to do all the things we thought we (ha!) might be exempted from. We're renegotiating our relationship to time. Who are we now? What are we supposed to do? Who are we supposed to be?

I think about mid-career writers. We aren't the writers we used to be, which is likely a good thing, but we also have had to surrender some ideas of what our futures can hold. We've had to adapt (note that *adapt* does not mean "give up"). Mid-career writers are building the bridge between the writers we were and the writers we can be.

I'm also drawn to the middle of the body. It's a place kept hidden. We may want it to be smaller. We may want stretch marks to go away. We may be refiguring how to dress to hide the new flesh. My belly fat. My squishy abdomen. My love handles—you name it.

The middle of a writing project brings up many similar associations. Questions of "What next?" or, "I'm supposed to go where?" surface here. The mythologist Joseph Campbell's concept of middle age as the time in life when we get to the top of the ladder only to realize we're up against the wrong wall can also apply to our work-in-progress. "I did all this work on my book only to find out there's a fatal flaw in my dramatic arc? Good heavens, does it have to be this hard?"

Let's shift connotations a bit and consider a middle as a passage, something that connects two separate places. A tunnel, a bridge, or a footpath. In the body, the fascia is the soft connective tissue that holds the whole structure together. It's our web of sticky proteins that keeps everything where it should be, providing tension and movement as necessary. We can think of the middle of a book as the connective tissue between the innocence of the beginning and the wisdom of the end. It holds everything together. Without the middle, the ends collapse. It provides a thematic container for the entire book. In the middle, the questions that were raised in the beginning come to full fruition. We start to understand the real stakes of the story. We see what the character has to lose. Indeed, without this middle of connective narrative tissue, we can't get our protagonists to the other side. There can be no transformation without the alchemy of the middle. As writers, we must pause for this uncertainty, so we will take the risk and make the changes needed to move forward.

You've reached a point in your development—either with your craft or with the personal aspect of your writing world—where it's time to take a step forward. Sometimes such steps are gradual. Sometimes you're dragged kicking and screaming into the next thing. Sometimes you resist until you can't stand resisting anymore. Sometimes it feels like all you're doing is changing, and then there's that nice lull when you might dare to think, "Oh my, have I arrived?" But there's no arrival. This is a lifelong journey; the only destination is the next word. Your middle may arrive a few days into your first committed writing practice. It may arrive after your first draft. It may arrive a dozen times during a project or even during a session. Normalize this place. Become at ease with and familiar with your body's responses to this place, this time when you need to learn something new. Try something unexpected. Shake yourself up. As you grow to recognize your body's responses to moving forward, you can normalize them.

You've been here before: there is another side.

DEEP INQUIRY PRACTICE
The Middle Muddle

When you consider the middle space, what do you think of? Write down everything that comes to mind—include words and images. If you'd like a starting line, try one of these:

» When I'm in the middle, I . . .
» The middle means . . .

To make meaning of the middle, start by looking at it and interacting with it through soft eyes. The time you spend writing in your

journal about your associations with the middle creates an awareness of current story lines and associations you may unknowingly
be attaching to "middleness." It's important to be able to say, "I am in
the middle," without falling into the story (the meaning) you may be
attaching to that. For example, "I'm in the middle of my life"—which
can mean "I haven't lived up to my potential," "I will never find true
love," and so on—is an example of living in the story of the statement
instead of the direct experience of it. It's the meaning attached to an
experience that can cause suffering. The only direct experience here—
the only thing you can actually claim—is that you're in the middle.
End of conversation. That statement alone doesn't create stress. The
meaning you attach to it is where the challenge comes in. Pay attention
to the stickiness of the stories you hold about things. They can bind
your feet if you cling to them.

Who's In There?

When you reach a block in your writing, tease out what voices come
into play. Who do you hear? What are they saying? How do you talk to
yourself as a writer, and what do you say about your work-in-progress?

When you find yourself stuck, write down exactly what's in your
mind. Transcribe your thoughts as quickly as possible. Get them out
of your head and onto the page. Do this each time you get stuck. It
may be helpful to have a separate section of your journal for these
transcriptions. Do you notice any patterns? Any similarities among
voices? If a voice makes multiple appearances, who might it be? Give
it a name. Start to uncover who is carrying on in your subconscious.

25 | Connect with Your Body

Our entire body is in the business of transformation. It is constantly changing, constantly taking one element in and transforming it into something else. From the air we breathe to the food we eat to the children we create, we take in, transform, and release. That's what bodies do. Gather, create, and release. The creative process is a natural part of being alive. We don't have to look outward for it. It's with us all the time. We just forget sometimes. We leave our bodies behind. We create a false separation between our bodies and ourselves.

Take a moment and close your eyes. Do a quick scan of your body using your inner vision. Use your breath to expand into areas of tightness and tension. Do you notice any places you don't want to visit? Any places you feel disconnected from? Keep the breath steady and full. Keeping your eyes closed, consider all the things your body does for you, much of it without your having to give instructions. It quietly goes about the business of keeping you alive. What a marvelous thing. Offer gratitude to it. Don't focus on what it isn't or what it can't do. Honor what it can do and what it is doing. Don't pay any attention to what you don't look like. Fall in love with what you do look like. Your body allows you to live. It holds the tools for you to read and write. To imagine. To travel. To love. To grieve, and to touch. Embrace all of it. Your stories are written on it.

Returning to the body helps us reconnect with the source of our work and helps us touch a part of ourselves that is always creating. Always churning. Always circling and spiraling. Always engaged in myriad activities that keep us moving forward. Paying attention to the body helps us tune in to these natural rhythms. Our creativity doesn't reside in the intellect. It lives in the body, and the body's cycles and processes show us how it works. We make things all the time. Returning to and consulting with our own forms can help nudge us back to flow.

DEEP INQUIRY PRACTICES

Embracing the Belly

This activity is accessible to everyone. If you are pregnant, you may wish to use the attention of your mind to massage your belly energetically rather than apply pressure to your body.

You can do this activity sitting, standing, or lying down. Take a moment to settle into your body and chosen position. Take a few deep, relaxing breaths, feeling your belly expanding on each inhalation and releasing on each exhalation. Relax your belly. Make sure you're not trying to hold it in. That doesn't serve you. When you're ready, begin to massage your abdominal area. Make small spirals with your hand in a clockwise direction as you move around your abdomen. Take your time, remembering to breathe. When you encounter areas of tightness, slow down the movement and breathe into the tight space. Soften your belly with each exhalation.

We can experience many energetic blocks in the abdominal region. Taoists believe that this area contains the essence of the human spirit. When we are blocked in the belly, that stress stagnates and festers, causing an imbalance. The navel center is our power center—the place where we store and transform energy. We can be our own most powerful and potent healers through abdominal massage. You can use this exercise as a warm-up activity to your writing practice or at any time during or after the practice.

If you want to add a focused meditative component to it, start by sitting in a comfortable meditative position, hands resting on your lower *dantian*. As you relax into your breath, let your mind loosely journey into your work-in-progress. Approach it with a sense of curiosity and wonder. What do you notice about the setting? Do you hear any characters' conversations?

With your eyes closed or with your gaze softly focused at a point a few feet in front of you, use active imagination to let yourself travel through your story until you find a door. When you reach the door, begin your abdominal massage practice. Let your fingers spiral naturally clockwise as they move around your belly.

Step through the door. Remember to breathe. Notice images, sounds, colors, smells, and characters that may surface as you enter the new space in your work. Continue to relax your belly. Keep your gaze soft and your breath easy and full. It may be helpful to have an audio recorder handy so you can say what you're observing as you move through the meditation. Then you'll have an easily accessible record of your journey without having to break the massage and meditation to get a pen. When you've completed the circle around your abdomen and your inner journey into the world of your story is finished, return to stillness with your hands resting on your belly, breath expanding your body fully, and releasing completely on the exhalation. Offer gratitude to your body and to your writing for the experience.

Writer's Portal Press

You can do this activity sitting, standing, or lying down. Using the index finger and thumb of your right hand, massage the webbing of flesh that lies between the index finger and thumb of your left hand. Using your thumb, probe the flesh until you find the point that's sensitive to pressure. When you find that area, press it twelve times. Switch hands when you're finished. Remember to breathe deeply during this activity.

This area is known as the "valley of harmony" in the Taoist tradition. Stimulating this pressure point will send energy through your arms and into your head. It helps to stimulate the flow of energy to your hands, which are the writer's tools.

Energy Washing

Stand in Tadasana (Mountain Pose), or sit in a chair with your feet touching the floor. Rub your palms together to create a nice heat.

Place one palm on your belly and use the other to "brush" down the opposite arm from shoulder to fingertip. You can lightly touch the arm or hover a short distance above the skin. Imagine moving the tension away from your shoulders and neck down to your fingertips and then dispersing it away from your body. Switch arms and repeat the activity on the other side.

26 | Make Friends with Stress

Writer's block creates stress, right? Or is it the other way around? Does stress create writer's block? Or is it all one giant circle, no beginning and no end, that will forever govern your writing life?

Here's how it works. You're moving right along and then, bam! You're not. You've stopped. You worry. You may never find the groove again. You have a deadline. You knew you shouldn't have had that slice of pizza last night. You're never going to make this thing work. The book is stupid. You're stupid. Let's give this whole thing up.

Stop right there. Let's examine for a moment what stress is and how it can serve you. Yes, I said how stress can serve you. Hang on. Stay with me for a moment.

Stress is the body's natural attempt to cope with its current circumstances while keeping itself alive. The body's primary goal is to keep itself functioning. Anything else, as they say, is gravy. Stress is one way the body communicates with itself. Stress gets a bad rap in today's world. We read article after article about how to eliminate stress from our lives. We're told stress is a factor in many deaths and illnesses. But what we're not told is how stress is actually a helpful tool to keep us moving in the right direction. It's a signal to us to pay attention. We may need to jump out of the way of that saber-toothed tiger. Since we rarely have to dodge saber-toothed tigers these days, our stress is more often linked to our expectations of what our lives are supposed to be. We more frequently create our own stress over things far less worrisome than being mauled by a tiger. Work anxieties, relationship anxieties, and personal pressures all contribute to the modern-day stress we hear so much about. Many of us engage in what's called *anticipatory stress*—we worry about what has not yet happened. That's a far cry from reacting in the present moment to a real physical threat.

The thing is, our bodies evolve slowly. We may have unimaginable technology and access to safe food and water like never before. But our stress hormones still can't distinguish between worrying about a blind date and outrunning an erupting volcano. So our physiological response to what is nonthreatening (at least on a physical level) is still at the heightened reaction of a life-and-death threat.

The body's natural fight-or-flight response is triggered by the stress hormones we release when we feel threatened. The sympathetic nervous system gets excited and tries to help us out by altering the body's physiological responses so we can move quickly. Heart rate increases. Blood pressure increases. Digestion slows. We're getting ready to run. This response, designed to keep us alive in case of a direct and present threat, can appear when we're sitting calmly at our desks putting words on paper. Hence, we pop out of the chair and get out of the room. There was no literal danger. But the body thought there was, thus causing us to react out of proportion to the moment. We responded physically to approaching something unknown in our work. We don't know what's there. Maybe whatever it is has been hiding for years. Maybe we don't remember putting it there. Maybe it's too much to look at. We got close to that unknown— the potential cornerstone of our work. We knocked at the door, but then we turned away. After all, it might house a saber-toothed tiger.

Eustress

The endocrinologist Hans Selye first used the term *eustress*. It refers to the positive meaning a person makes of a particular stressor. Eustress puts us to work growing rather than fleeing. It's the stress that helps us be better, the stress that reminds us to study so we'll perform well on a test. It's the stress that motivates us to discover new things, advance in our field, make positive changes in our lives.

Eustress creates a challenge that makes us use our resources (both internal and external) to achieve the goal we've set for ourselves. It's the stress we may experience while watching a scary movie (which allows us not to actually experience what's in the scary movie). It's the stress that makes us achieve things and keep stretching just a little bit further. It's also known as "positive stress." The idea is that we need some stress to do anything at all. Some kinds of stress are actually positive motivators.

The challenge in modern life is to distinguish between the stress that requires a fight-or-flight response and the stress that is simply urging us to keep going, to try something else, to become better. When we're in our offices or coffee shops writing our books, odds are good we aren't in imminent danger.

DEEP INQUIRY PRACTICE

Trigger Moments

Getting a handle on our trigger moments in our writing sessions is very beneficial. Much like an addict wants to understand what triggers addictive behavior, writers can benefit from paying attention to what triggers their stress responses when they're working. The trigger moment is also called an *antecedent*—that which comes before the reaction. We can learn a lot about our behaviors when we understand what occurs before our stress response. For example, if you are trying to lose weight, you might first notice that you frequently eat in the middle of the night. If you take that awareness a step deeper, you can look at what you might have been thinking about or doing before going to the kitchen. If you keep a log of those antecedent moments, you can, over time, look for patterns that can help you make adjustments.

Notice Your Responses

How do you experience the stress response in your body when you're writing? Think about physiological reactions as well as other kinds of reactions (checking e-mail, looking at Facebook, and so on). Once you've identified reactions and responses, begin keeping track in your notebook of what you were doing or thinking just before the reaction occurred. Were you thinking about a breakup with your significant other? Were you worried about an Amazon review? Were you concerned about what would happen at work tomorrow?

You may find this level of awareness and attention difficult to achieve at first. Most of us are not accustomed to such precise observations of our own behavior. Keep a log over several weeks or months before you try to ascertain patterns. No day is the same. You may not even remember what you were thinking about before the behavior. You just noticed the behavior. That's a powerful first step. Be patient with yourself as you deepen your relationship to your patterns. Observe without judgment. You're not doing this to condemn yourself. You're doing this to grow.

Bring It On

Write a scene in which you are about to engage in one of the activities you listed in the previous practice that causes you some stress. Really embody the scene. You may want to begin your descriptions at the ground and move up. Beginning a scene's creation from the lowest physical level of the setting can help to ground you in that scene and place. Let yourself slip into your skin at that moment of stress. You might want to close your eyes for a few minutes and imagine one of these moments. Don't worry about getting yourself too worked up. The writing will help bring you back to center.

Focus on the physical manifestations of the stress in the body of the character you've created to represent yourself in this situation. It's perfectly fine to make things up. What would you *imagine* the character might be feeling? Be specific. Focus on the physical sensations of anxiety and don't get hung up in any meanings that follow them. Can you move even deeper and find the specific moment those feelings intensify? What is happening right before the tension spikes? Write the scene *forward*—let you-as-the-character move all the way through the arc of the feeling—from before the event takes place through the moment and to the other side. Stay in the imaginative realm of the character's body as you move through the scene. Remember, this isn't about the perfect scene that will fit in your book. This is about using writing as a vehicle for self-exploration.

When the scene is complete, practice three rounds of Balancing Breath to bring you back to the current place and time and to release any residual anxiety you may have built up.

Learn More

Psychologist Kelly McGonigal's TED talk, *How to Make Stress Your Friend*, is a great introduction to reframing your perceptions about stress. She addresses how stress, when viewed through a positive lens, is actually good for you, and how it encourages you to reach out to others.

27 | Sit with Discomfort

We've been taught to move away from what is uncomfortable. This is absolutely logical and serves us well when the discomfort is physical pain. When you put your hand on the stovetop and it's hot, the pain is your signal—your teacher—telling you to move your hand *right now*. People who suffer from rare genetic disorders that prevent them from feeling pain have to be extremely careful because they don't know that they've touched a burner, broken a leg, or gnawed their tongue to shreds as they were grinding their teeth. Pain lets us know we need to do something different. The pain itself is rarely the problem. The pain is signaling the problem (touching the hot stove). Pain tells us to pay attention.

When we're writing, we are not (we hope) in physical pain. Our work, however, can ignite emotional pain and discomfort, internal signals to pay attention. These emotional attention grabbers will trigger the same response as physical pain. Get away! Now! Move away from whatever is causing this sensation. This is a time when many writers play what I like to call the Deflection Game. Here's how it can show up: You're writing along merrily. All is well. What a great writing session today! Then you hit something unexpected in the work. "What's that? Oh dear, is it *that*?" You don't want to look at that right now so you will do one (or more) of the following:

» Check e-mail	» Clean the house	» Drink something
» Check Facebook	» Turn off the	» Call someone on
» Go shopping	computer	the phone
» Go to the gym	» Eat something	» Text everyone

None of those activities are problems in and of themselves, but when they are behaviors you use to deflect from what is in the present moment, they can be less than helpful. When you can identify your primary methods of deflecting from the work at hand, it is easier to make modifications. These deflections happen in seconds, and until you start really paying attention to when and how they appear, you may not even notice you're doing them. The writing is trying to take you somewhere, and it scares you on some level. It awakens something you may not have known was there or may not want to look at. That's normal. That's what writing does. It's calling you, raising you up, asking you to wake up to something. And that something is connected to the questions that got you involved in your project in the first place. The emotional and psychological discomfort is a clue that you're reaching somewhere with untapped potential. It's helping you connect the dots. That emotional discomfort feels like physical discomfort too. For some people, it's a clenched jaw or contracted breathing; for others, it's a headache or an upset stomach. It's helpful to pay attention to how your own body responds to emotional tension. When you're in a tense place, your whole body is saying, "Hey! I've got something to say! Please listen!"

Our bodies are not just bones and blood. Our inner world is also a component of our physical form. The mind and heart's signals are as vital and necessary to our well-being as the signal to get our finger out of the boiling water. Begin to notice your methods and your body's responses. Do you experience wet palms? A dry mouth? Rather than deflect, which will quickly turn into writer's block, hang around a little. These signals are important. They're asking you something. Sitting through the discomfort, much like holding a yoga pose longer than you might like, will show you there is another side that you'd never have found if you had walked away.

DEEP INQUIRY PRACTICES

Get Grounded

At any time during your writing practice, you can take a quick break and reconnect to the earth and your foundation. Come to standing. Root the four corners of your feet to the floor. On an inhalation, raise your arms over your head. On an exhalation, bring your palms together and lower them to your chest in prayer position. Pause and take a full inhalation and exhalation. On the next inhalation, separate your palms; on the exhalation, slowly fold forward toward the floor. If your palms won't touch the floor, lower yourself gently to your knees and then press your palms to the floor. If you're not able to lower yourself to the ground, you can modify the pose by sitting in a chair and pressing your palms on the desk in front of you as you exhale.

Hand Massage

Mindfully massage each of your fingers, taking time to pay attention to any areas of stiffness or tightness. Don't try to pop or crack your knuckles! Massage into your palms and the backs of your hands. You may want to offer gratitude for all the work your hands do each day—not just writing but in every area of your life. It may be helpful to free-write, describing the hands of a character you're having difficulty accessing. What was the last thing that character's hand touched?

Bumblebee Breath

This is a simple and powerful activity to help clear your head, relieve minor sinus pain and headaches, calm your emotions, and rechannel your energy. It is also called Bhramari Pranayama; *bhramari* is a type of Indian black bee. To practice Bumblebee Breath, sit up straight in a comfortable position. Softly close your eyes and bring a slight smile to your lips. Place your index fingers on the cartilage between your cheek and ear. (This is what you would likely press if you wanted to close off your ears from a loud noise). Don't put your fingers *in* your ears. When you're ready to begin, inhale deeply and exhale fully to clear your body, and then take your first-round inhalation through your nose. On the exhalation, release the breath, keeping the lips closed, with a high-pitched humming sound. You can press and release the cartilage between your cheek and ear, or you can keep it pressed lightly. Breathe in again through your nose and exhale with another high-pitched hum, remembering to keep the lips closed. Continue for six rounds.

28 | Venture into Unknown Waters

As writers we must be willing to go where we haven't been before. We have to be willing to discover and uncover parts of ourselves that have been hidden away—for all types of reasons—and to keep peeling back our masks until the face of our work shines through, unobstructed by shadows and attachments.

Imagine what courage it took for explorers in the Middle Ages to venture out into the ocean. They set sail with the most meager of supplies—no GPS, no satellite phone, no refrigeration. Still, they set out, as human beings have always done. Our curiosity wins. All kinds of motivators push us to strike out into the unknown. Writing is this type of ocean voyage. Your curiosity pulls you forward into a place you haven't yet been, and it dares you to follow.

Writing a book is also an express train ticket to your deepest self. And chances are, you have some things down there you've put away for a reason—and more than a few things you've no idea about. Writing takes you into these places because the writing is what's calling to you *from* those places. That whisper, "I've got something to say," that makes you open your journal is coming from your deepest self. It's calling you, direct from the depths of your subconscious, and you are brave enough to pick up the phone.

The ferocity of the resistance you may feel when writing about a certain thing is directly proportional to the necessity of the work. When you're moving deeply into something, your inner "guards" may rise up fast and furiously to keep you from getting any closer. The patterns that manifest are connected to the themes of the work you're creating. Pay attention to what shouts within you. It's pointing you toward thematic gold. Remember that your writing is urging you forward. It's ahead of you on the path. Return to a place of trust. Follow the words. Don't fall prey to patterns of the past or succumb to familiarity. Notice what you feel, but don't let resistance direct the show. Instead, let it inform the work.

Navigating the murky waters of the unconscious can be frightening. It's easier to skate on the surface, not really touching anything that will make a difference, not really shifting anything of substance. It may be easier to keep things safe, but that won't stop the whispers or quell the desire to write stories that impact the world. Eventually, we all must be willing to go deep, be vulnerable, and show ourselves something unexpected. This takes courage, but it's worth it. Your courage spills over onto the page and into the lives of others. Take the risk. We're waiting for what you bring back.

DEEP INQUIRY PRACTICE

Here Be Monsters!

Back in the day, cartographers mapped out the world's oceans as they understood them, often writing on the black, unknown waters of the map, "Here Be Monsters." Create a map of your writing process in this format. What are the continents in your writing process? Where are the oceans? The unknowns? The monsters? Don't just point to where the monsters are. Name them. Draw them. Find out who's living in your writer's ecosystem.

Writer's Energy Ball

This exercise is based on a fundamental tai chi practice that is often used as a warmup and to help practitioners develop sensitivity to the powerful energies contained in the body. This activity helps you cultivate and channel energy into your hands. As writers, whether we handwrite or type, our hands are the primary body parts we use to create our art. This body-based activity can help stabilize and ground you when you're working with your inner monsters.

Begin by standing, keeping your body relaxed. Your spine should be straight, your shoulders relaxed, your jaw loose, and your tongue resting in the center of your mouth. (You can also touch the tip of your tongue to the back of your front teeth, if you prefer. There's a natural resting place for it there.) Take care not to lock your knees. Imagine your feet are connected to the earth with strong, flexible cords of energy.

Bring your palms together in Writer's Mudra. Take a deep breath in, filling your belly. Exhale fully. You may want to offer an intention, a question, or an affirmation to your writing. If you're working on a specific challenge in your work, you may want to ask a question related to that challenge. Whatever you offer, when you're finished, let that offering dissolve.

Rub your palms together to generate heat. When you feel the heat rising, slowly separate your palms a short distance, keeping them facing each other. Feel the warmth stretched between them. Slowly separate your palms a bit more, then draw them back together, but don't let them touch. Do this several times, feeling the warmth of energy pulsing between them. You may notice this energy as a resistance between your hands.

Begin to mold this energy into a ball with your cupped palms. You can play with this energy ball by slowly stretching your palms apart and bringing them back together. You can roll the ball in your hands by rotating the positions of the left and right palm from top to bottom. Keep your mind focused on the energy between your hands. Soften your gaze. Remember to breathe. As you hold the energy ball, allow images, words, feelings, and questions into your mind. Let them wash through you. Don't attach to any of them. Be present with what is arising.

When you feel complete, bring your palms slowly back together in Writer's Mudra. Place your palms over your lower belly, the *dantian,* and breathe deeply into the warmth in your abdomen.

When you feel ready, you may want to move to your journal to follow the threads that arose for you during the moving meditation.

29 | Have Faith

The writing process comprises many things—patience, discipline, study, apprenticeship—but at no time do those amorphous elements of faith and trust come into play more than when you're feeling stuck. This is not faith in a deity or a set of religious tenets, but faith in the things that brought you to the page itself, and a trust that the work can help carry you when you're not sure what to do. When you can't see a way forward but are too far gone to turn back, you can throw up your hands and check in with your companions: faith and trust. Return to faith in yourself and the reasons that brought you to the project in the first place. Remember, even if finishing that book is just for you, the work still has great value. Whether a book is published or not has little impact on its value to its author. Your work is somehow helping you, even if you can't yet see how.

When you're stuck, it's beneficial to return to the beginning of your book to find a new or renewed understanding of what the work's intrinsic value might be. What was the problem or question that pulled you to the story? Has it changed? Is it no longer relevant? If not, then maybe the story has already done its work for you. Only you can decide. But in times of chaos, don't forget that the book called to *you*. It pulled you toward it. What was powerful enough to get you out of your regularly scheduled life and make you turn to the solitude of the page? Those answers can be touchstones to help you remain grounded when you don't know where you're going. You can feel secure in how you came to be there. Navigating a block requires a deep trust that even if you can't see the other side, you will find a way there. This trust is an inner fortitude. Use the beginning of your project to help anchor you and build a bridge across the great divide.

When you can remember where you've been, it's easier to get where you're going.

Faith and trust are also helpful friends when we take the road less traveled in our drafting process. To grow a book and to grow as a writer, we have to be willing to not always know where we're going. We can't be afraid of a detour, even if it turns out to be a dead end. Fortunately, many writers come equipped with the ability to use *cognitive disinhibition*. This term simply means that we do not ignore things that don't seem relevant to the current goal. We might think of it as having an open mind. Anything can come in. Anything may be relevant. Those false leads? They could be the path to the heart of the story. Cognitive disinhibition may even be at the heart of the aha moment, which is certainly not an instant bolt of lightning from the sky but rather the result of many attempts that did not produce anything (except, of course, the attempt that did).

People who exhibit strong cognitive disinhibition understand the importance of exploring roads where they can't see the destination, and they trust each path they take will provide them with *some* insight if not *the* insight or awareness they were hoping for. Once we decide on an answer or a single solution, our minds close out the other paths and focus only on what will lead us to and support that answer. This isn't "bad"; it's actually a pretty awesome adaptation tool for this crazy life. But it's not a tool best suited for all stages of the creative process. We have to gain more skill at using the right tools for the job—not the same tool for every job.

Deep Inquiry works like a spiral, not a direct line. We spiral, like a snail's shell, deeper into our work and ourselves. We backtrack occasionally, visiting the same areas with different feet and eyes. We sometimes seem to spin in place. But each move takes us a little deeper in. Trying to take a direct route—going head-on at a problem—can sometimes make us freeze even more. It can feel aggressive, too intentional, too convinced of an outcome, too urgent. We need the insight of what came before in order to take the next step. We move question by question, just like we move from one word to the next, until we reach the resolution (which will likely not be a solution but rather a shift in perception). Don't be surprised if your questions yield similar responses or themes as you practice. We have our trunk of hauntings—our issues and passions that fuel a lifetime's worth of writing. What a gift, to be so haunted.

DEEP INQUIRY PRACTICES

WWW Practice

This practice plays off our understanding that "www" is a gateway to an address on the Internet. We can use this idea to create "addresses" for our work-in-progress. We write word + word + word = WWW.

There are a few ways you can work with this practice. You can pull three random words out of your word bag, place them on the top of a page in the order you pulled them out, and use those words as a starting point for a free-writing session. Or you can take each word on its own and create a scene that surrounds the word. Or you can think of literally joining them together, like boxcars on a train, and add the fourth word intuitively. For example, if you have *wagon + raven + grass,* the fourth word might be *Kansas.* There's obviously no right answer. This practice helps train your intuition (which was already hard at work gathering words for your word bag) and helps you make unexpected associations. You can surprise yourself. You may not know what Kansas has to do with your book yet, but it's a step you can follow. See what you can uncover. This activity also helps you learn to trust yourself and cultivate cognitive disinhibition, the ability to accept all possibilities during the creative process without needing to select one as better than the other.

Tic-Tac-Toe for Writers

Draw a tic-tac-toe board. Each of the squares represents an aspect of your work-in-progress. Place a question from the place where you're stuck in the center and fill in the other boxes from there. I've created a sample one here.

Character	Setting	Emotion/tone
Line of dialogue	Dramatic question of the scene	Conflict of the scene
What came before the scene	Character's primary yearning	Antagonist's yearning

When you've completed the board, write a scene that encompasses all nine elements. You can use this tool anytime you feel stuck. It simply helps you to approach the scene from a different angle. Sometimes head-on is the least effective route forward. Feel free to create your own catagories for the squares.

30 | Devote Yourself to Your Writing

Always remember what draws you to the page. What calls you to devote so much time and energy to the pursuit of the art of writing? The word *devotion* is rooted in the Latin verb *devotio,* meaning "to love, to serve, to give yourself over to." This heart-based word can help us when we contemplate opening ourselves up to our work. The people and things we devote time and energy to reflect that time and energy back to us. What we give energy to will grow. What urges you to apply this level of care and nurturing to writing?

There's a profound connection between devotion and discipline. What we love, we commit to. What we commit to, we come to love and understand on a very deep level. What we come to love will show us everything. What we come to know gives us everything.

If you choose writing as one of your acts of devotion, prepare to be a student of its wisdom as long as you show up for its gifts. Writing will pull you forward into places you can't yet see. It will bring with it the challenges you need to become more fully alive and awake. It will bring with it the obstacles you need to grow.

DEEP INQUIRY PRACTICE
Devotion Dive

For what other areas of your life do you hold devotion? Perhaps for a child? A pet? A garden? Another hobby? How do you make time and maintain energy to care for these other aspects? What might you be able to learn about how you care for something other than writing that you can then apply to your writing relationship?

Write a letter of recommitment to your writing or project. Some couples do a periodic reassessment of their relationship commitments. Try something similar for your writing relationship. What's working for you both? (Don't forget to ask your writing and listen to what it tells you!) What adjustments can you make? How will you hold up your end of the commitment? The in-between space is a great time to reevaluate what's working for you in terms of your practice and what you can fine-tune. We always need to maintain flexibility. This kind of inquiry helps you cultivate yourself as a good steward of your work. It's the routine maintenance necessary to keep anything you value—from your home life to your job performance to your writing—in good working order.

Making Connections

> » Why am I here writing now?
> » How does my writing serve me?
> » How does my writing serve others?
> » What tangible benefits does writing bring to my life?
> » What intangible benefits do I reap from writing?

Writing is a long game. Train and maintain accordingly.

PART THREE **Beyond the Block**

If you surrender to the wind, you can ride it.

—Toni Morrison

31 | Embrace the Re-Vision

How do you know when you're done with a draft or with a whole project? We hear stories of authors who revise their work at a book-signing event while actually holding the published book. How, then, can revision ever be complete?

The hyphenation of *re-vision* in the chapter title is intentional. You are in the re-vision stage, literally reseeing your work. This book isn't focused on revision, but because revision is an essential part of the writing process, *and* because the thought of revision frequently causes writers to panic, I want to reframe some of the elements and offer you some tools to approach this essential part of the process.

» Revision is necessary for *everyone*. You're not the superhuman special person who doesn't need to do it. What a relief!
» Revision is one of the ways you uncover the art of your book.
» Revision is an exploration into the deeper heart of your work. It's not a slash-and-burn, take-no-prisoners approach. It's a pruning, a replanting. A reconception of your book that occurs *naturally* as you get to know your story.
» Approach revision with compassion and softness. Be open to what the next stage will show and teach you.
» Revision isn't a failing. It means you've got the understanding of a pro. You're willing to do the necessary work to serve your art.
» Revision is not editing. A re-vision—or reseeing—is not yet sentence-level tinkering. It's looking at the big picture. Editing occurs after you've done enough drafts to know you've got the structure—the bones of the book—where you want them.

The best analogy for revision I've found comes from Janet Burroway in her classic textbook, *Writing Fiction*. She says that revision isn't the rearranging of furniture in a room. It's taking everything out of that room and then deciding what belongs in it and what may need to be added. The process of taking everything out of the room is the blank page for your second draft. You won't see all that was there so you won't be so determined to make everything you see somehow fit.

The ending of a draft and the end of an entire project are similar, respectively, to the freshman and senior years of high school. After freshman year, you have a sense of where you may be going and what you might have to do in the years to come and what will be expected of you, such as two years of algebra and a semester of Spanish, but you don't know *for sure*. You might have to move during your junior year. You might experience a family tragedy. You might lose focus on school and get wrapped up in other things. You have windows of possibility, but you haven't made it to the prom. You've heard about the physiological changes that are coming (puberty)—ack! Lots of firsts are still on the horizon, but you haven't experienced them yet. They're all potential futures, not elements of the past that you can agonize over in therapy for the rest of your life. At the end of freshman year, you know there's more to come.

At your high school graduation, you know you're beginning an entirely new phase of life. Yes, there's still more to come, but it isn't going to be connected to high school—the characters, setting, and responsibilities will be different. You're continuing to move forward, but you know you're entering another story. The end of a book feels more like this experience. It's time to go. You just *know*.

I don't know when your work is done. Your teacher or writing group can't tell you either. Only you can ultimately make that determination.

DEEP INQUIRY PRACTICES

Clean Slate

If you're between first and second drafts, try this: reread the first draft as quickly as you can (no scratching things out!). Then put it aside and start fresh in a new document or notebook. Why? This is not the time to wrestle the perfect sentence to the ground. Our brains are master puzzle solvers. A draft is a puzzle—a problem to be addressed and solved. If you tinker with the first draft as you see it, your brain will do everything in its power to use the parts in front of it. It is much more difficult to allow for necessary growth and new input in the next draft if your eyes see only the first draft. Your mind will work with what it believes it must to solve the problem. But that first draft wasn't a problem. It was just a first draft. Don't be afraid to start again. You won't lose anything. A first draft's only job is to exist. Once it's in the world, its duties are complete. Use it as the springboard into what's next. Let it be the foundation from which you build the book. *It is not yet the book.*

How Do I Know When I'm Done?

When you feel you may be at the end of a whole project instead of a draft within a project, ask yourself a few things:

» **Has the book answered its own questions?** Has it fulfilled its promise to the reader? If yes, yay. If no, you're not done.
» **Has the book answered *my* questions?** Has it fulfilled the reasons that drew you to it, reasons of which you may not even have been aware? If yes, and you aren't looking to go public, you are likely done. If you do want to go public, then see the preceding question.
» **Is the craft as impeccable as I'm currently capable of delivering?**

Keep in mind that there is no end to learning what writing can do. When writers are revising from published work, it's because they've figured out something new that they didn't know when they wrote the original. That's normal. That means they're engaged in lifelong learning about their art. You will *always* find things you can make better. But at some point, you have to let it loose. People with perfectionist tendencies have a great deal of difficulty here. Your work will always be capable of growing. Don't hold a draft back from your agent or editor while you wait for perfection to arrive (it never does). The healthy side of a perfectionist tendency is represented by the diligence and care that you take with your work. You're not sloppy. You honor the reader and the work by taking your time with it. The shadow side of perfectionism tends to eviscerate a work—after all, it will never be "good enough." Working to create the best book you can is healthy and noble. Expecting that it should and will be perfect takes an honorable act and turns it toxic.

Getting Clear on Your Feelings

If you have negative, challenging, or intricate feelings about revision, do a separate Deep Inquiry process around this stage of the process. You can start with this baseline prompt: What connotations do I attach to revision? Make an uncensored list. When you're finished, choose one of the feelings to work with. You might like to personify it. Then continue with this prompt: What do I mean by _____? Fill in the blank with the feeling you chose. Follow that train of thought and see where it takes you. This exercise gives a deep bow to Linda Metcalf and Tobin Simon and their book, *Writing the Mind Alive*.

Hidden Meanings

You can also try an exercise to help you identify a false belief or "shadow" that you hold about revision that will help you move through it. Use these prompts:

» If I revise my work, I will . . .
» If I revise, it means that . . .

32 | Pause between Drafts

Yay! You made it through a draft.

Crap! You made it through a draft.

It's not over. Not yet. You know this, and it both excites and terrifies you. Whether you're between drafts of a single manuscript or have just finished the final draft of one and are waiting for the next project to knock at the door, the in-between space is a great time to revisit some of the foundational practices and feelings you have about writing and the project itself. It's also a great time to "wash that draft right out of your hair" so you can regroup and recommit. Take care not to drag your draft with you. Don't worry (easier said than done, I know!) about what you have left to do with the work—what you didn't do, what you should have done—there's plenty of time to get back into it. But for now, close the door (and really close it!).

Kinesthetically, you can pace out a boundary for yourself—a reclaiming of your space and a separation from the work-in-progress. You also give your work a boundary when you do this. Your book needs time away from you as much as you need time away from it. Don't keep picking at its new flesh right now. Let it be. A stalked manuscript never comes to its fullest fruition. Space is essential to its unfolding.

Maybe you want to go as far away from your work as you can. Maybe you've had absolutely enough of it for right now. Or maybe you're anxious to dive back in and "fix" everything. Neither of these extremes will be helpful at this point. Everything needs to breathe. Your work is no exception. Everything needs space to find its center again. Just like we need the white space along the edges of a page to frame the text so it can be read, you need to hold that space for your work when it is between drafts.

Have you ever had one of those manic moments when you solved all your problems (and everyone else's) in the middle of the night, only to find all the flaws in your genius plan in the stark light of day? We all allow our emotions to get the best of us and direct our actions at times. Finishing a writing project frequently comes with a lot of emotion and different feelings. Feel them, but let them pass through you right now. In the flush of finishing, don't upload your book immediately to Amazon or iBooks just because you can. (Don't make me repeat that one!)

It used to be necessary to wait. The options available to writers just ten years ago required time. You couldn't finish your draft at midnight and have it available for sale in the Kindle store the next morning. Now you can. And while many of the new publishing options are good for authors and help us not be utterly dependent on an increasingly "megaseller-only" publishing model, the new world order demands that we impose a bit of self-control. We need to regulate our impulses.

Consider the relationship between the urgent impulse to get this done or published now and grasping and striving for a specific result. How might it be linked to an attachment to a particular outcome? We may want the result we've dreamed about—we may even have envisioned a particular way for that result to occur—and come hell or high water, we will make it happen. Who needs to revise? Revision is for others. I beg you, don't make that mistake.

Consider the flip side. You may experience a sudden timidity and vulnerability now. "Oh my goodness, let's just stop right here. Let's pretend I never did this. No one has to see it. No one has to know. I can't put my work out there ever, ever, ever, because _____. I'm afraid of being seen? Of being found out? Of having to claim once and for all that I *am* a writer?" These thoughts and many more have pushed writers back into self-imposed silence. Don't let that happen to you.

At the beginning of a meditation practice, students frequently experience a great deal of resistance. They often come to the mat seeking a specific outcome (such as reduced stress, some sort of promised enlightenment, lower blood pressure), as if these things were commodities that could be acquired by sitting—some sort of transactional exchange. Then the practice starts, and quiet starts to creep in. Who knew it would be so silent? Who knew how much effort we put into avoiding that silence and finding activities that distract us from our inner world? The intensity and volume of that inner world can throw the best of us off course when we take the time and space to connect with it. What's in there? How badly does it want to communicate with us?

Rather than turn our backs on the pause, which is a natural part of the writing process, let's move into this necessary space of silence between drafts or projects. Remember, fields must go fallow before they can be replanted. That's healthy. It takes time and space for things to reveal themselves.

DEEP INQUIRY PRACTICES

Breakdown

Get a pen and paper. What do you need to do in your next draft to move the project to the next level? Go. Write down everything you can think of. It doesn't matter how absurd. Just get the thoughts out of your head. Then separate them into categories such as Plot, Craft, Character, and Research. Which ones do you feel you know how to do? What do you still need to learn? Choose one skill from those you still need to learn. What steps can you take to learn that skill or find that answer? Put the action items in your calendar. Do this with as many steps as you want.

What we're doing here is breaking things down into manageable, actionable items so you won't feel so panicked. Defining terms and outlining next steps really do help create clarity and a greater sense of ease about what to do next. When everything is just swimming around in your head, it's difficult to know how or where to begin. This can cause physiological stress responses and send you into a fight-or-flight mode.

Fine-Tune Your Feelings

Get a pen and paper. What feelings are you having about your current draft? Write them all down. Keep things uncensored and raw. When you're finished, choose one that feels particularly potent for you right now. Begin a Deep Inquiry Dialogue with that feeling. Ask the feeling, "What do you need? How can I help?" You might also inquire into the *nature* of that feeling. What does the feeling mean to you? Where is it manifested in your body? Where has it shown up before? You can also create your own questions. Make sure they are open-ended to allow for connection and exploration rather than closed questions that require only a yes-or-no, right-or-wrong answer.

33 | Welcome the Silence

Whether you're between drafts or at the end of a long-term project, there's no avoiding that sticky space in between. The place where the voices in your head get really loud, and you wonder if you are indeed as crazy as they've always said you are. This time in between is as dangerous a passage as adolescence. Everything sounds like a good idea because it keeps you from just being still with what is. "I know!" the inner adolescent may say. "Let's get drunk and go boating!" Or, "Let's go shopping and spend every cent we have on white T-shirts." Or, "Let's borrow half a million and open a bricks-and-mortar shop that sells only orange ceramic pots!" Gosh, everything sounds so perfect and brilliant. How will you choose?

The real distractions, of course, are not the traffic noises, the loud neighbor, the television, or the Internet. The real distractions are internal. The discomfort inside is what ultimately makes us get up from the chair and turn away from the work. Writing is an active thing. It's also an art that requires deep focus and a willingness to dive into the inner workings of our hearts. We'll frequently opt for the distraction excuse when we hit something real. When we hit something with juice. It's easier to abdicate our responsibility by passing off the reasons for leaving our work onto something external. The drive, discipline, and devotion to writing come from within. They get challenged from within and they get embraced from within.

When the silence has grown loud in your writing life, let the thoughts in but allow them to pass through, unencumbered by your attachments. They are only thoughts. They arise and dissolve all on their own. When you can't shake a thought, it's because you haven't let it leave your grasp. The next time you find yourself attached to a thought, smile, inhale deeply, and blow that thought away. It's only hanging on because you are.

DEEP INQUIRY PRACTICES

108 Luminous Breaths Meditation

Sometimes it's helpful for a meditation practice to have a mantra. The mantra is simply a way to anchor the mind when it starts to fly off into the stratosphere, as the mind tends to do. In this practice, the mantra is the counting of breaths. Find a comfortable position sitting either on the floor or in a chair. Ground yourself into the energy of the earth through the soles of your feet or the backs of your thighs and sit bones. Relax your jaw and tongue. Soften your gaze. Take three deep, cleansing breaths. When you're ready to begin the meditation, just breathe at your normal rate and depth. Don't try and manipulate the breath. After each complete breath (inhalation, pause, exhalation), count that breath. After your first complete breath, you'd count "one"; after the second, "two"; and so forth. When you lose count or forget to count, return to the beginning, starting over with one. The cycle is complete when you've counted 108 breaths without having to start over.

Stillness Meditation

Sometimes a mantra is not at all helpful. People attach too much to doing something "right." They feel they must say the right things, sit the right way, clear the mind, envision something, or release something according to the rules. That attachment sabotages a practice that is meant to help us detach and be with what is. In this meditation, don't worry about anything—not counting, not sitting a certain way, not chanting, not manifesting, not releasing, not anything at all. Be still and soft. Allow the world to keep moving around you as you remain in stillness. As thoughts arise, let them surface and let them dissolve. When noises occur—birds, phones, people talking—don't attach to the sounds. Let them in and let them out. The noises won't distract you from meditation if you're not attached to the need for silence. You're simply an active observer in everything. As sensations arise in your body, notice them and soften into them. Unless you're in pain, just be with what's happening. The internal body is very busy! Practice Stillness Meditation for fifteen minutes, working up to longer sessions as you feel ready. If you like, have your journal ready to free-write when you're finished.

For a different approach, instead of doing this once a day for fifteen minutes, try it three times a day for five minutes, and observe the differences and similarities between the two approaches.

Heartbeat

Find a comfortable place to sit and settle into silence. Let your breath fill your center, belly to clavicle, and soften your body. Place your right palm over your heart and focus on your heartbeat. Remaining still and silent, let your fingers themselves hear the beating. As your attention keys in on this rhythm, stretch it out into your entire body. See if you can feel the pulsing in your wrists, ankles, and behind your knees. Surrender your whole body to the beat. You may wish to record this experience in your journal.

Quick Tips

These additional exercises may help jump-start your writing by taking you on unexpected side routes. Sometimes, when we take roads less traveled, we find the way home.

» Write a letter of gratitude to your draft.
» Write a letter of invitation welcoming in the next draft.
» Read something utterly unrelated to your work.
» Rearrange a room.
» Call someone on the phone.
» Clean out and organize your writing space. Take everything out of the room if you can, and make conscious choices about what to bring back in.
» Take yourself out on a creative date, or schedule a creative

retreat in which your focus is on something *other than* writing. Exploring other art forms feeds your own.

» Take the time to read John Steinbeck's journals on the writing of *East of Eden* and *The Grapes of Wrath*. They provide deliciously funny, insightful, and illuminating descriptions of the nuts and bolts of the writing process. Look for *Working Days: The Journals of* The Grapes of Wrath and *Journal of a Novel: The* East of Eden *Letters.*

34 | Say Yes to the End

My mother was a transplant from New York to North Carolina. She grew up going to theater events and did everything she could to instill a love of theater in my sister and me. It worked for us both. My first professional writing gig was for the stage. There's something about the once-in-a-lifetime magic that is created when a group of people come together to produce a show. It's never the same from night to night. A performance is a communally produced singular work of art and, much like Tibetan monks' sand paintings, the physical representation of impermanence.

In high school, I fell even more in love with theater. I worked on every show I could. We held two productions a year—big ones, with music, dance, drama, sets, lights, and costumes. When I figured out my acting ability was never going to get me cast, I decided my natural control freak tendencies and organizational prowess would be excellent to ensure that everything about the show ran as it should, so I stage-managed everything from freshman year forward. For four years, I had a group. A place I belonged. A community. I learned how art could work by participating in how it was constructed. The magic that appeared when the audience arrived was never diminished by an understanding of how we put it all together. If anything, the magic was that much more remarkable because something unpredictable and alive was created anew each evening. Something emerged that was far greater than the individual parts that held it together.

But closing nights always made me melancholy. Our group was dissolving. Many would be graduating. The day after we closed the show, known as strike day, was when we dismantled our work. We dusted away our sand paintings. We took everything down, stored the sets, repainted the stage floor to black, and washed costumes. We cleaned the makeup room; rehung the lights back to a neutral wash; navigated some drama among friends (it was high school after all). Then the theater, where we had lived and cried and kissed and fought and struggled with lines and choreography for nine weeks, looked as if we'd never been there. Strike day was the day of erasure. We were wiping our own slates clean. We really didn't know what to do with all the time before the next casting call. All that empty space. All that energy put into making something—moving *toward* something—that was over quite anticlimactically. We whimpered out. I don't know what I thought there should be instead of the whimper. A brass band finale? Someone who profoundly understood what we had done to say, "I saw what you kids did. You *made* something together. There is nothing more sacred on earth"? That never happened, of course, but I looked for it.

When you finish a writing project, something that took you so much time, something that you have come to know perhaps more intimately than anything else in your life, it is—in its current incarnation—over. And you're alone. You and your writing. No brass band. Maybe someone is waiting for your work. Maybe not. For the moment, you aren't actively making anything. And for artists in any field, that's an uncomfortable place to be.

I offer this to you: Say yes to this ending, one ending out of many. Sit with it. Honor where you've come from and where you might go next. It's OK to feel sad. Relieved, even. This time is just another moment and movement in the writing process. It's necessary. Don't run from it. Don't try to fill it. Don't jump right into a revision. Give yourself time to breathe. To do something else. To take time to gain necessary perspective. You *and* your work need this time. This time is a bit like doing that juice cleanse you've been putting off or that engine flush for your car. Or as a more yummy example, think of it as the requisite cooling time for a pan of piping hot brownies. Things are still happening with your work even if you can't see it. Magic is still simmering. Don't rush the alchemy.

DEEP INQUIRY PRACTICE

Separation Practice

Begin by joining your palms in Writer's Mudra. Rub them together to generate heat. Then slowly separate them, feeling the energy stretching between them like taffy. Envision your separation from this draft or project as you dance with the energy field. When you've stretched as far as you want, flick your fingers, snap your fingers, and then clap your hands three times.

Build Your Ritual

Endings are times of celebration and acknowledgment. We graduate from school. We complete a draft of a book. Create a ritual that marks this stepping-stone on your path. Honor the work you've done with gratitude, and offer an invitation to what is coming next.

Afterword

In closing, know that there is no closing. There is a limitless amount of unfolding you can do as an artist and a human being. I hope you will use all the tools from this book in other aspects of your life. You can create questions specific to your current dilemma and use them to help you make decisions—to help you make a choice about the next project, the next job, the next move.

Ask. So much is waiting to be said to you. Don't look for the answer; rather, seek to deepen the questions. Use this book and its tools as a springboard for where you will go next—the next step, the next sentence, the next kiss. Soften. Release. Listen.

Thank you.

Acknowledgments

No book comes to life fully formed all on its own.

The practices I've offered build on the broad and sturdy shoulders of many seekers, scholars, and artists, including Machig Labdrön, Carl Jung, James Pennebaker, Louise DeSalvo, Lucia Cappaccione, Linda Metcalf, Tobin Simon, Ira Progoff, Gestalt therapy, and the Bonny Method of Guided Imagery. I've listed sources and references at the back of the book for those of you who may wish to delve deeper into some of the practices and techniques. Not only is it respectful and important to honor our ancestors, but it's a professional courtesy as well. We're all in this together, each adding a new perspective to the larger conversation.

Deep gratitude:

To my agent, Linda Roghaar, who has believed in me and my work for twenty years. No matter how many editors reply to her, "I'm not sure we could sell this book," she keeps sending my proposals out until we find the one who does believe in them—and in me—as much as she does.

To my husband, Keith, who has spent the better part of his midlife listening to me talk about writing and teaching and stories. He makes my work and my life better every single day.

To my writing partners, Gayle Brandeis and Michaela Carter. Thank you for what you give to me by simply being who you are. Here's to us!

To the Kripalu Center for providing the space and the students that help me become a better teacher.

To my students, whose questions force me to try and find solutions. You help me grow.

To my editor, Jennifer Urban-Brown, and the team at Shambhala. Thanks for continuing to believe in the power of writing to transform.

To Cain Carroll for friendship, long conversations, and insights about the body and movement I'd never have found on my own.

To Jeffrey Davis for helping me move into the next place, and to Hiro Boga for recalibrating my relationship with my work.

I am always and forever grateful.

Powersheet 1:
Proposed 49-Day Writing Schedule

For each day you plan to write, indicate the following: time (such as 11 A.M.); duration (such as 1 hour, 2 hours, 15 minutes); and location (such as office, coffee shop, car, park).

1 _____

_____

2 _____

_____

3 _____

_____

4 _____

_____

5 _____

_____

6 _____

_____

7 _____

_____

8

9

10

11

12

13

14

15

16

17

18

APPENDIX: POWERSHEETS | 163

19 _____

_____

20 _____

_____

21 _____

_____

22 _____

_____

23 _____

_____

24 _____

_____

25 _____

_____

26 _____

_____

27 _____

_____

28 _____

_____

29 _____

_____

30 _____

_____

31 _____

_____

32 _____

_____

33 _____

_____

34 _____

_____

35 _____

_____

36 _____

_____

37 _____

_____

38 _____

_____

39 _____

_____

40 _____

_____

41 _____

_____

42 _____

_____

43 _____

_____

44 _____

_____

45 _____

_____

46 _____

_____

47 _____

_____

48 _____

_____

49 _____

_____

Powersheet 2:
Actual 49-Day Writing Schedule

For each day you *actually* write, indicate the following: time (such as 11 A.M.); duration (such as 1 hour, 2 hours, 15 minutes); and location (such as office, coffee shop, car, park).

There's no judgment here. Just observe what you do and when you do it. Use this tool to help you find a schedule that works *for* you and *with* you rather than against your personality and your life's current demands.

1 _____

_____

2 _____

_____

3 _____

_____

4 _____

_____

5 _____

_____

6 _____

_____

7 _____

_____

8 _____

_____

9 _____

_____

10 _____

_____

11 _____

_____

12 _____

_____

13 _____

_____

14 _____

_____

15 _____

_____

16 _____

_____

17 _____

_____

18 _____

_____

19 _____

_____

20 _____

_____

21 _____

_____

22 _____

_____

23 _____

_____

24 _____

_____

25 _____

_____

26 _____

_____

27 _____

_____

28 _____

_____

29 _____

_____

30 _____

_____

31 _____

_____

32 _____

_____

33 _____

_____

34 _____

_____

35 _____

_____

36 _____

_____

37 _____

_____

38 _____

_____

39 _____

_____

40 _____

_____

41 _____

_____

42 _____

_____

43 _____

_____

44 _____

_____

45 _____

_____

46 _____

_____

47 _____

_____

48 _____

_____

49 _____

_____

Resources

Contemplative and Body-Based Practices

Carroll, Cain. *The Four Dignities: The Spiritual Practice of Walking, Standing, Sitting, and Lying Down.* London: Singing Dragon, 2014.

Chia, Mantak and Maneewan. *Chi Nei Tsang: Internal Organs Chi Massage.* Chiang Mai, Thailand: Healing Tao Center, 1990.

Esterly, David. *The Lost Carving: A Journey to the Heart of Making.* New York: Penguin, 2013.

Loori, John Daido. *The Zen of Creativity: Cultivating Your Artistic Life.* New York: Ballantine Books, 2005.

Tharp, Twyla. *The Creative Habit: Learn It and Use It for Life.* New York: Simon and Schuster, 2006.

Writing as Exploration

Barry, Lynda. *What It Is.* Montreal: Drawn and Quarterly, 2008.

Bayles, David, and Ted Orland. *Art and Fear: Observations on the Perils (and Rewards) of Artmaking.* Eugene, OR: Image Continuum Press, 2001.

Davis, Jeffrey. *The Journey from the Center to the Page: Yoga Philosophies and Practices as Muse for Authentic Writing.* 2nd ed. Rhinebeck, NY: Monkfish Book Publishing, 2008. (You can find out more about Jeffrey's work at http://trackingwonder.com.)

DeSalvo, Louise. *Writing as a Way of Healing: How Telling Our Stories Transforms Our Lives.* Boston: Beacon Press, 2000.

Metcalf, Linda, and Tobin Simon. *Writing the Mind Alive: The Proprioceptive Method for Finding Your Authentic Voice.* New York: Ballantine Books, 2008. (You can find out more about Linda and her work at http://pwriting .org.)

Moore, Dinty W. *The Mindful Writer: Noble Truths of the Writing Life.* Somerville, MA: Wisdom Publications, 2012.

Pennebaker, James W. *Opening Up: The Healing Power of Expressing Emotions.* New York: The Guilford Press, 1997.

Pressfield, Steven. *The War of Art: Break through the Blocks and Win Your Inner Creative Battles.* New York: Black Irish Entertainment, 2012.

Progoff, Ira. *At a Journal Workshop: Writing to Access the Power of the Unconscious and Evoke Creative Ability.* Rev. ed. New York: Tarcher, 1992.

Hero's Journey and Myth
Campbell, Joseph, with Bill Moyers. *The Power of Myth.* New York: Anchor, 1991.

Vogler, Christopher. *The Writer's Journey: Mythic Structure for Writers.* 3rd ed. Studio City, CA: Michael Wiese Productions, 2007.

Writing Craft
Brooks, Larry. *Story Engineering: Mastering the 6 Core Competencies of Successful Writing.* Cincinnati: Writers Digest Books, 2011. (You can find out more about Larry's work and follow his incredibly helpful blog on story and structure at http://storyfix.com.)

———. *Story Physics: Harnessing the Underlying Forces of Storytelling.* Cincinnati: Writers Digest Books, 2013.

Burroway, Janet, Ned Stuckey-French, and Elizabeth Stuckey-French. *Writing Fiction: A Guide to Narrative Craft,* 9th ed. New York: Longman, 2014.

Cron, Lisa. *Wired for Story: The Writer's Guide to Using Brain Science to Hook Readers from the Very First Sentence.* New York: Ten Speed Press, 2012.

Gutkind, Lee. *You Can't Make this Stuff Up: The Complete Guide to Writing Creative Nonfiction—From Memoir to Literary Journalism and Everything in Between.* Boston: Da Capo Press, 2012.

Kooser, Ted. *The Poetry Home Repair Manual: Practical Advice for Beginning Poets.* Lincoln: University of Nebraska Press, 2005.

Kowit, Steve. *In the Palm of Your Hand: The Poet's Portable Workshop.* Thomaston, ME: Tilbury House Publishers, 2003.

Pattison, Dorothy, and Kirby Larson. *Novel Metamorphosis: Uncommon Ways to Revise,* 2nd ed. Little Rock, AR: Mims House, 2012.

Rainer, Tristine. *Your Life as Story.* New York: Tarcher/Putnam, 1997.

Watt, Alan. *The 90-Day Novel: Unlock the Story Within.* Los Angeles: The 90-Day Novel Press, 2010.

Websites and Online Resources
Association of Writers and Writing Programs
   www.awpwriter.org
   A community, opportunities, ideas, news, and advocacy for writers and teachers of writing.

Lynda Barry
   http://thenearsightedmonkey.tumblr.com
   Linda's incredibly rich Tumblr blog that contains exercises, videos, music playlists, and all sorts of amazing insights into the creative process and the

world of the image from her multidisciplinary course at the University of Wisconsin–Madison.

Hiro Boga
http://hiroboga.com
Business strategist, transformational teacher, and energy alchemist.

Jennifer Louden
http://jenniferlouden.com
Author, teacher, and inspiration.

Mark Matousek
www.markmatousek.com
Award-winning author, teacher, and contemplative.

Poets and Writers
www.pw.org
A magazine, an online database, and all-around goodness for writers at all stages of their careers.

Writer's Digest
www.writersdigest.com
The online presence of *Writer's Digest* magazine.

About the Author

MH RAMONA SWIFT

Laraine Herring directs the creative writing program at Yavapai College in Prescott, Arizona, and works as a premium consultant for Tracking Wonder in the Hudson Valley of New York State. She is also Head Monkey at Fierce Monkey Tribe. She holds an MFA in creative writing and an MA in counseling psychology. Visit her at http://laraineherring.com and http://fiercemonkeytribe.com.